# Servant-Minded Leadership

## *How Mindfulness Changes Servant Leadership*

By
Jon Antonucci

# Dedication

This book is dedicated to all the forgotten leaders doing the best they can with what they have and changing the world, one person at a time, despite rarely getting any of the recognition they deserve or the empowerment they need.

I see you, I hear you, and this book is FOR you.

# Foreword

I am delighted to write the foreword for my friend Jon's book about servant-minded leadership. The idea of Servant Leadership goes back to Jesus, who had a mindset of humility and servanthood. Servant Leadership came to the forefront with Robert Greenleaf's essay, *'The Servant as Leader'* in 1970, and has become a mantra in many leadership books since then. The problem is that becoming a servant and leading are antithetical ideas, for when we become leaders, we also have to guard against the pride and power that accompany leadership positions. Enjoy this book, and I challenge you to lead with a servant's heart.

Leadership is often associated with power, authority, and influence. Yet, the most transformative leaders in history—the ones who leave a lasting impact—serve first. Servant Leadership is not merely a strategy or technique; it is a mindset, a way of being that prioritizes the growth and well-being of others. It is about lifting people up, not positioning oneself above them.

In a world that increasingly values profit over people and efficiency over empathy, the principles of Servant Leadership stand as a beacon of hope. This approach fosters environments of trust, collaboration, and genuine care. Whether in business, education, government, or community service, servant leaders create cultures where people feel valued, heard, and empowered to reach their fullest potential.

However, leading as a servant is not easy. It requires humility in a world that rewards pride. It demands patience in an era of instant gratification. Servant Leadership challenges the notion that success is defined by titles, wealth, or authority. Instead, it calls us to measure success by the growth of those we lead, the strength of the communities we build, and the integrity with which we lead.

One of the greatest challenges of Servant Leadership is that it often goes unrecognized. In a culture that celebrates charismatic, dominant leaders, the quiet, selfless work of serving others can feel thankless. Servant leaders must be willing to make difficult decisions for the greater good, even when it means personal sacrifice. They must be strong enough to absorb blame and wise enough to give credit where it is due.

Despite these challenges, the rewards of Servant Leadership are profound. When leaders prioritize service over self-interest, they cultivate stronger teams, increase engagement, and drive sustainable success. Employees are more loyal, communities are more resilient, and businesses thrive—not merely because of financial gain, but because they operate with purpose and integrity.

This book is an invitation to embrace a different kind of leadership—one that is rooted in humility, compassion, and a commitment to the greater good. It challenges us to ask: *How can I serve? How can I make those around me better?*

Whether you are a CEO, a teacher, a coach, or a parent, the lessons in these pages will inspire you to lead with a servant's heart. The world needs more leaders who understand that true greatness is found not in being served but in serving others. May this book guide and empower you on that journey.

**Brent D. Garrison, Ph.D.**

**President Of *By The Book Consulting***

# Introduction

I didn't start out as a great leader. In fact, it could be (correctly) said that, in the early years of my leadership experience, I was a downright terrible leader. I certainly wasn't a servant leader... and was even less a Servant-MINDED Leader. If I were to be transparent about my early days in leadership, I didn't really care about anyone except myself. Of course, I would pretend to care—as long as my ego was gratified, and my ideas were propagated. But it was purely selfish and was anything except love-based.

Thankfully, over the years, I have learned a thing or two about both myself and the calling of a leader, and I would love to share this with you! Now, you may be asking, *"Another book on leadership, Jon?"* Well, not exactly. I mean, technically, yes, but the goal might be different. There are certainly a number of books on leadership—many by authors who are smarter, more experienced, and probably more qualified to write them. So what in the world do I have to offer in a conversation that has been so widely covered?

First of all, this is a book for leaders. This means it aims to respect the thing you have the least of: time! I know how busy you are. I know that you want to read and grow. I also know that there are only so many hours in the day! So, we are going to make this book short, sweet, and to the point. We are also going to break it up into smaller chapters so that if you only have three minutes between breakfast and rushing out the door, you might be able to get a little bit of inspiration for the day! And, if you don't have time for a full chapter but want to head to work with some empowering words, check out the leadership concepts summary pages that start on page 134. They will summarize the contents of each chapter and provide you with relevant, impactful ideas that you can implement TODAY!

Second, I think that there are a TON of great concepts pertaining to leadership that are out there, but I have also come to see a glaring gap in leadership conversations. I see a lot of leadership materials that are oriented toward the organizations to which they are sold to. But I see precious little relevant info that is intrinsically helpful to the leaders themselves, and especially the front-line and middle management leaders. Most of what I see is more theoretical than practical, and very little of it directly applies to the daily responsibilities and frustrations of leaders who are working directly with staff.

Now, while it could be said that my contribution is somewhat semantical, I would counter that it is very practical. And, it is my hope that, as you read this book, at least 3 things will happen.

1. You will be challenged to re-evaluate the way you currently think about leadership in general—and Servant Leadership, in particular.

2. You will be inspired to be the best leader you can possibly be!

3. You will receive practical tools that will empower you to effectively engage with your team.

As previously mentioned, this book is for leaders—regardless of what position you hold (or if you even hold an official leadership title). Whether you are a formal or informal leader, you are a current or aspiring leader, or you are vastly experienced or just emerging as a leader, this book is for you. BUT if you are a front-line leader, one who is working directly with the staff of an organization, this book is **especially** for you! My passion is to empower you because I know that very few of you are being given the resources that you need to succeed in the position that you have been given. And, if you are one who is not technically in a position of leadership but have noticed that people are often placing leadership responsibility on you, then I commend you for picking up this book, and I promise you will get MASSIVE value from it.

# Table of Contents

+

# Section 1

## *The Original Concept of Servant Leadership*

I have never liked reading books that spend the first 100 pages trying to convince me the book is necessary. So, I want to avoid that as much as possible. However, to effectively share the value of Servant-Minded Leadership, we are going to have to spend a few minutes talking about the OG of the leadership development world: good ol' Servant Leadership.

The idea of "Servant Leadership" is not new. The phrase became popular in mainstream business conversation after Robert K. Greenleaf published an essay, "The Servant as a Leader," in the 1970s. But the concept is found in other writings that are thousands of years old. Furthermore, Servant Leadership has been modeled by the most successful leaders for as long as history has been recorded.

In this first section, we will look at the roots of Servant Leadership, including its origins, the individuals who made it popular, the positive impact it has had, and we'll close out the section with my predictions of Servant Leadership.

# *Chapter 1*

## *The Original Idea of Servant Leadership*

*"True leadership is not about being in charge; it's about serving those in your charge."*
— ***Simon Sinek***

With the exception of the following (italicized) section, this book was written without the help of AI. However, for the purpose of providing an amalgamized summary of what Servant Leadership is, I could think of no better way to obtain such info than to ask an AI, "What is the general idea of Servant Leadership?"

The AI bot had this to say:

*"Servant Leadership is a leadership philosophy and approach that emphasizes the leader's primary role as a servant to their team, organization, or community. This concept was popularized by Robert K. Greenleaf in his essay "The Servant as Leader" in 1970."*

*The general idea of Servant Leadership revolves around the following key principles:*

1. ***Priority on Serving:*** *A servant leader's main focus is on serving the needs and well-being of their followers. They prioritize the growth, development, and success of their team members.*

2. **Empathy and Listening:** *Servant leaders are empathetic and actively listen to their team members. They seek to understand the perspectives, concerns, and ideas of others before making decisions.*

3. **Commitment to Growth:** *A servant leader is committed to the personal and professional growth of their team members. They provide opportunities for learning, skill development, and advancement.*

4. **Building Relationships:** *Servant leaders foster strong relationships based on trust, mutual respect, and open communication. They create a positive and supportive environment where people feel valued.*

5. **Ethical and Moral Behavior:** *Servant leaders adhere to high ethical and moral standards. They lead by example and make decisions that are in the best interest of their team and organization.*

6. **Shared Decision-Making:** *Servant leaders involve their team members in the decision-making process, considering their input and ideas. This participatory approach promotes a sense of ownership and responsibility.*

7. **Empowerment:** *Servant leaders empower their team members to take ownership of their work and contribute meaningfully to the organization's goals. They provide autonomy and support to encourage creativity and innovation.*

8. **Service to the Greater Good:** *Servant leaders recognize the importance of contributing to the well-being of the broader community and society. They aim to make a positive impact beyond their immediate organizational responsibilities.*

9. **Humility:** *Humility is a core characteristic of Servant Leadership. Leaders prioritize the needs of others over their own ego, demonstrating humility and selflessness.*

10. **Long-Term Perspective:** *Servant leaders focus on the long-term success and sustainability of their team and organization, rather than short-term gains.*

*"Servant Leadership stands in contrast to more traditional, hierarchical leadership models where leaders often wield authority and control. Instead, servant leaders view themselves as facilitators and enablers, working to create an environment that supports the growth and well-being of their team members. This approach has been embraced in various fields and is considered a valuable way to promote collaboration, employee engagement, and organizational success."*

Not bad, huh? For the most part, I appreciated the summary that the chatbot provided. But I do have one matter of disagreement with the implication of the first paragraph. While it does say that it was **"popularized"** by Robert Greenleaf, which technically acknowledges he got his idea from somewhere, I think that there is a lot of value in mentioning how long Servant Leadership has been around.

In fact, the original idea of Servant Leadership can be found long before the 1970s, when Robert Greenleaf wrote his essay. Check out some of these quotes from leaders who are much older than just a few decades:

*"Those who will be great among you will be a servant."*
**Jesus of Nazareth (AD 20)**

*"The role of the leader is to create the environment in which all members of an organization have the opportunity to realize their own potential."*
**Aristotle - Nicomachean Ethics (340 BC)**

*"(There are) three styles of compassionate leadership: the trailblazer, who leads from the front, takes risks, and sets an example; the ferryman, who accompanies those in his care and shapes the ups and downs of the crossing; and the shepherd, who sees every one of his flock into safety before himself."*
**Buddhist tradition**

What do you think? Do these sound as much like Servant Leadership to you as they do to me?

As you can see, the ideology of Servant Leadership has existed for a lengthy period of time. During this time, the principles have not changed much at all. All leaders who have subscribed to and lived out this powerful philosophy have demonstrated that leadership that serves the best interests of the ones it leads is the most positively impactful to both its followers and the overall world.

The principle of Servant Leadership rests on the foundation of human dignity and intrinsic value. It bucks against the ego-centric tendency of domineering leadership and repels the stench of fear-based or position-oriented leadership, which is more interested in one's own prestige and accolades than the success of their team.

> *"Leadership that serves the best interests of the ones it leads is the most positively impactful to both its followers and the overall world."*

Servant Leadership, in its purest form, is centered on the opportunity for a leader to positively impact the lives of those around them through empowering and loving influence that supports individuals in a way that allows them to become their best selves.

What an amazing concept, right? Anyone who does NOT agree with this form of leadership should probably just put this book down now. Because I promise you, while I AM going to contrast this definition with what I consider a higher form of leadership, we are NOT debunking it. We are only adding to it, not subtracting from it.

In our next chapter, we will look at some of the more contemporary voices of Servant Leadership and their impact on many modern lives.

# *Chapter 2*

## *The Personal Impact of Servant Leadership (1970s and Beyond)*

*"A true leader is one who empowers others to rise, fostering an environment where everyone can thrive."*
— *John C. Maxwell*

I don't know why this is, but it seems like we are often more interested in what people from a long time ago had to say. The older the quote is, the more veracity it seems to have, probably because it is more time-tested and thus considered to have endured more scrutiny. Therefore, in the first chapter, we looked at the ancient voices and the ideology of Servant Leadership from long ago.

Now it is time to bring it to a more modern era and look at some of the loudest voices in the Servant Leadership conversations over the course of the last half-century. While there are many people who could be named, I will only name a few and will invite you to reflect on your own experiences to suggest more in your mind. The goal is not to nominate all of those with influence in this area, nor is it even to bring up the **"best"** voices of the modern era. Rather, I simply aim to reference some of those who have helped to shape the conversation around leadership in the recent past and who may be familiar, regardless of whether one has studied leadership in the past or not.

In no particular order, I think of John Maxwell, Dale Carnegie, and Simon Sinek. There are some who might suggest that Tony Robbins and/or Gary Vaynerchuk, Steven Covey, and others should also be included in this list. While I agree they certainly could be, again, the point is not to name every person who is having success as a leadership expert. But I do want to drop two names that you may have never heard of. (If you haven't, I would recommend them both highly as fantastic modern examples of dynamic leaders.) Brent Garrison and Matt Scott are two individuals in my life whom I have been privileged to work with and for, who are the embodiment of Servant Leadership.

Nevertheless, without getting into the weeds, if I could synthesize everything that I have learned from these modern voices and examples of leadership, it would be summed up in one sentence: *Leadership is not about the leader; it's about the team.* This sentiment is widely accepted as the philosophy of Servant Leadership, and it is espoused by many of the most prolific voices of the modern era.

> *"Leadership is not about the leader; it's about the team."*

It is from this place of reason that we see books, webinars, speeches, events, and a myriad of other forms of dissemination promoting this idea in various forms. From employee wellness programs to leadership development initiatives, most of the content centers around the idea that deference should be given to the team, and the leader should be their biggest champion and advocate.

Some things that I have caught from each of the names listed above (again, this list is NOT exhaustive) include:

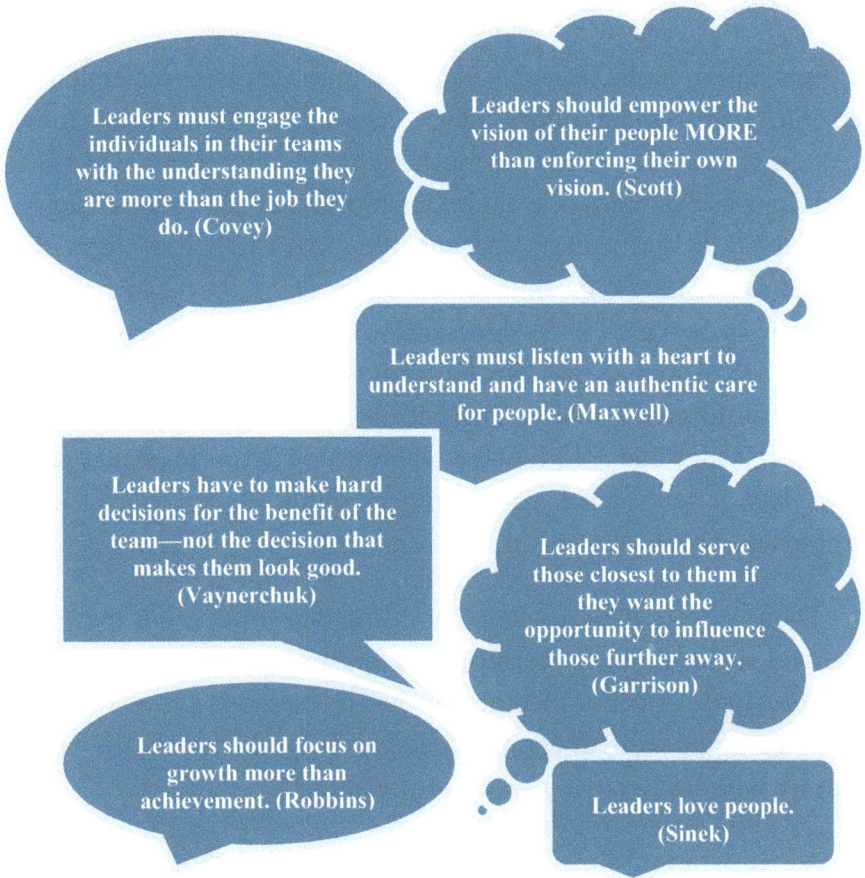

Leaders must engage the individuals in their teams with the understanding they are more than the job they do. (Covey)

Leaders should empower the vision of their people MORE than enforcing their own vision. (Scott)

Leaders must listen with a heart to understand and have an authentic care for people. (Maxwell)

Leaders have to make hard decisions for the benefit of the team—not the decision that makes them look good. (Vaynerchuk)

Leaders should serve those closest to them if they want the opportunity to influence those further away. (Garrison)

Leaders should focus on growth more than achievement. (Robbins)

Leaders love people. (Sinek)

Pretty good, huh? Of course, this is not everything these individuals have said, but these are some things I've caught from them. Maybe you have received something even more impactful. Either way, the value of their contribution has been fairly dynamic.

Through the voices of these individuals and many others, the message of Servant Leadership has been carried forward and has become even more of a household idea. Their books, podcasts, speeches, and other PR have given the average individual the opportunity to understand more about this powerful concept and have even made "Servant Leadership" a top search result on the most popular search engines.

In addition to the (mostly) famous names that I have mentioned so far, there is an entire other class of Servant Leadership representatives that we are not touching on. I briefly mentioned Matt and Brent as examples of great leadership. But mostly, we have only looked at the influencers. Meanwhile, MILLIONS of fantastic leaders are making a dynamic impact on the teams they lead via their example of Servant Leadership. And while we may not know their names, we recognize that they have impacted our lives! In my own life, I would give a nod to Elisabeth Waite, Angelica U., and my brothers, Caleb and Josh (another abbreviated list). I hope that you, too, have a few names that spring to mind when you consider examples of great leadership.

These leaders may not have world-famous voices, but they are the real world-changers because they are impacting lives directly, and the ripple effect of their actions has no bounds! This is the real message of the modern era of leadership. It is all about LIVING it! But we will discuss that in just a few chapters!

As we wrap up this chapter, having looked at those who have continued to perpetuate the Servant Leadership model, I hope you will walk away with the knowledge that Servant Leadership is not an old concept that was pioneered in the 70s and then left to simmer. No, it is a leadership theory that has taken root and is now carried forward by many others, who are relevant in the modern age, over 50 years later.

# Chapter 3

## The Positive Impact of Servant Leadership

*"Great leaders don't set out to be a leader; they set out to make a difference. It's never about the role, always about the goal."*
— ***Lisa Haisha***

The idea of Servant Leadership was clearly articulated in the 1970s and has been fairly well propagated by voices such as Carnegie, Covey, Maxwell, and Sinek into the 21st century. With the ideology seeming to have surpassed the bounds of generational relevance and transcended specific industries, we must ask a very important question. What has it changed? Maybe more effectively, we could ask, what has the impact of Servant Leadership been over the course of the last 50-60 years?

This is an interesting question because, depending on who you talk to, you may get different answers. If you were to ask an individual who has a current supervisor who has attended several leadership seminars but continues to cut down the team and micromanage their roles, you may hear the answer: "Not much!"

Similarly, if you connect with a person who is currently part of an organization that is operating as it was common in the industrial era, they would probably say that the past 60 years of leadership development haven't really hit the mark, as they haven't experienced any of the benefits.

Alternatively, if we asked someone working in tech in 2019, we might have heard a different story as they raved about how their company was going above and beyond to create a culture of empowerment, openness, and collaboration.

And somewhere in the middle, we might talk to someone who is not really sure about "Servant Leadership" but thinks that, when they get their next promotion, they might be more interested. Or we might come across one that has a good amount of knowledge on the subject but doesn't feel like they are currently in a position to put any of it into practice.

While if we did a survey, we might get six different answers from five different people, I think we would find a common theme. This theme may be the singular change that can be undeniably attributed to the impact of Servant Leadership over the last several decades.

What is the impact?

I think, if there is a singularly impactful aspect of Servant Leadership that we can see over the course of the past six decades, it is… the conversation.

The what?

The conversation.

It's the conversation that's changed. Whether we are talking to someone who is displeased with their boss, another who is supremely happy with their leader, or even one who wants to be a great leader, the difference is that there is *a conversation* about it. This will not always be the case. There was a time when leaders were *expected* to be jerks, and no one thought much of it.

I'm not saying that there was never a conversation about leadership or even how to be a good leader. As mentioned in Chapter

1, the concept of leadership—and even Servant Leadership—is not new. However, it was not a mainstream topic. It was not a subject that sold out conferences. It was not a topic that the average person felt they had the right or capability to engage. About all that anyone thought to do at that time was complain… and complain quietly so they didn't lose their job. But there was certainly satisfaction with the voices that dared to speak up, even if only vicarious satisfaction. I think of Dolly Parton's song, *9 to 5*, which captured the feelings of many people while simultaneously revealing there was no solution in sight. Maybe you thought of the more direct song by Johnny Paycheck, *Take This Job and Shove It*. Now, that's a pretty accurate reflection of how many people feel, even today!

Just like in the past, we live in a world of imperfect leaders (including you and me). Some are worse than others, but we all face the same reality that was not common a century ago: our leadership is actively compared (or contrasted) to an ideal that has been shared by those mentioned.

Whether we like it or not, we now live in a world that pressures us toward Servant Leadership. Despite the fact that we have a choice of how to respond, nowadays, we feel the pressure of leadership in a way that was not previously felt. While supervisors in the industrial era had to account for the output of their team (something we still get to do), they were not judged on things like employee turnover. There was no such thing as "toxic leaders" in the vocabulary of the average worker. But the conversation has changed. And believe me when I say that even the most crusty and resistant leaders are feeling the pressure to conform.

> *"Whether we like it or not, we now live in a world that actually pressures us toward Servant Leadership."*

13

I am fairly confident that, regardless of who picks up this book, whether you are a tenured leader or just entered the workforce, you probably didn't have to look up the term "Servant Leadership." If you did, I commend you for pursuing growth. But the reality is that most people will not need to do too much research on the topic because they are already at least generally familiar with it.

This is not to say that we have perfected the idea or that it is even well-implemented overall. In fact, I think we still have a long way to go when it comes to the implementation of Servant Leadership principles. However, it seems undeniable to me that the conversation has certainly shifted. That shifting of conversation has done a world of good. And I think that it will continue to yield positive results.

The more people are familiar with the concept, the greater the expectation will be that those of us who are leaders will lead well. That pressure will (hopefully) motivate us to step up, raise up other great leaders, and continue to make a positive change in the world.

Let's talk about that in the next chapter.

# Chapter 4

## The Lasting Impact of Servant Leadership

*"The greatest legacy of a leader is not what they achieve, but what they inspire others to achieve."*

— ***John Maxwell***

With the idea of Servant Leadership being firmly established in the modern work culture (albeit not always effectively implemented), we wonder how long the impact of Servant Leadership will last. Is it a temporary fad? After all, 60 years may transcend generations, but it is still a relatively short period of time. What will happen in the event of another recession, or worse, depression, that changes the work landscape?

Maybe another question we want to ask is, has it even worked? I hosted a webinar in early 2024 titled, *After 60+ Years of Training, Why Isn't Leadership Fixed Yet?* If you have worked with leaders who can spend all day quoting leadership experts like those previously mentioned in Chapters 1 and 2 but didn't seem to be so good at living it out, you may be wondering whether there has truly been an initial impact, let alone a lasting one.

I recall working for a particular leader who often cited great leadership thinkers like those I previously mentioned. And I think this leader genuinely considered themselves to be one who lived the values they had read about and spoken about. But if you worked for them, you quickly realized that the leadership strategies that were discussed were not particularly well implemented. If you have experienced something similar, you may feel like the idea of Servant Leadership having a "lasting impact" is something that is premature at best (and possibly downright naive at worst).

For the sake of this conversation, I would like to ask that we agree on only one thing. NOT that leaders are good at Servant Leadership. NOT even that leaders completely understand Servant Leadership. I ask that we agree that Servant Leadership, as a concept, has made a splash in the pond of professional experience and (if nothing else) has impacted what we expect from our leaders, even if it doesn't always impact what they offer. If we can agree to this simple (and admittedly one-sided) idea, I think we can proceed to engage the question of the lasting impact of Servant Leadership.

> *"Servant Leadership, as a concept, has made a splash in the pond of professional experience and (if nothing else) has impacted what we expect from our leaders, even if it doesn't always impact what they offer."*

So, returning to the question at hand, what does the future of Servant Leadership look like? Personally, I think it will continue to have an increasingly impactful presence in the professional world. I believe this for two reasons (other than my general optimistic outlook on life).

1. There is increasing support among both leaders and staff for the Servant Leadership model.
2. Servant Leadership has become extremely profitable (more on this in the next section).

With respect to the first point, there are an increasing number of people (both in leadership and otherwise) who are convinced that Servant Leadership is a superior art. Their evangelism is not likely to be quieted unless absolutely irrefutable data is obtained that unquestionably shows that Servant Leadership has had a negative result on business. And even if that were to occur, I think there would be people (like myself) who would STRONGLY question the source of the data.

This reality suggests that the ideals of serving the team first is not going anywhere. In fact, by sheer merit of the current momentum, it is realistic to suggest that it is likely to continue expanding in both influence and implementation.

Not only do people want leadership that genuinely cares about them and works to serve the success of the team, leaders want to be known as authentically caring individuals. Some leaders take this too far and try to be everyone's friend. This "Michael Scott" approach will be addressed later in the book. But the reality is that most leaders want to be seen as caring, effective, and overall "good" leaders.

On the second point, I do not want to get ahead of myself. So, for now, I will simply say it is obvious that the number of books, seminars, webinars, trainings, etc. that are centered around Servant Leadership make it incredibly difficult to let go of. This is both because those who are collecting the revenue from the paradigm are not likely to let the conversation die and because those who are investing the resources are not likely to admit they wasted their money on foolishness. So, you see, not only does the Servant Leadership philosophy have intrinsic merit and value, but even if it didn't, both sides of it (producers and consumers) would be unlikely to admit **"the emperor has no clothes"** because they both have too much at stake.

So, what will the impact be? I think this is actually the more important question. It's part of the reason I wrote this book. Ultimately, the answer depends on several factors:

1. Who controls the narrative?

2. What expectations develop?

3. Why people adopt the Servant Leadership rhetoric.

4. How the principles are implemented.

I intend to spend the vast majority of this book talking about how we can ensure that Servant Leadership (or what I call Servant-*Minded* Leadership) can have a dynamic, positive impact on the professional workforce. In this chapter, I will simply say that the impact (regardless of the answers to the above questions) will be positive.

Just as I indicated in the previous chapter, when I said that simply changing the conversation had a positive impact, I believe that as the conversation grows, it will only result in more positivity. Regardless of the intention or implementation of the Servant Leadership paradigm, there will be more conversation about it and that will improve the day-to-day working lives of those who have a leader they work for. Granted this is a pragmatic approach. Essentially, I am saying that, regardless of what happens, there is likely to be more conversations and thus development in the Servant Leadership space. This can't be all bad and will likely be good even if only in the long run or end.

So, as I wrap up this chapter, I think that the impact of Servant Leadership will not only continue into the foreseeable future but will also have a positive impact. I think that those of us who are advocates of this philosophy have a lot to be excited about. I think that those who have been subjected to poor leadership have much to expect. And I think that those who desire to be great leaders have a ton to look forward to.

# *Section 1*

## *Conclusion*

We've begun this book by looking at the amazing idea of Servant Leadership. We explored principles that have been millennia in the making. Did you know that Servant Leadership has been spoken of for so long? Many people are surprised to hear that writing, which dates back to the BC era, demonstrates that these principles were discussed and (in some cases) modeled by leaders of yore.

We also looked at the modern pioneers of Servant Leadership's current form. Names that we both recognize and have never heard of give us all a better understanding of what we as leaders are called to be. And we gratefully take inspiration from their words and examples. It is the examples that we can see with our own eyes that are likely to have the greatest impact on us.

Thankfully, the combination of Servant Leaders, both old and new, has had an amazing impact on the professional landscape. If nothing else, they have helped to change the conversation. There is now an underlying question that exists in most organizations asking whether the leader is a good (servant) leader or a dinosaur that needs to level up. This was not always the case, but it is a welcome change!

And, with all of this in mind, we're excited about the future. The outlook of leadership and Servant Leadership in particular looks bright! There is very little to suggest that its influence or impact is likely to diminish any time soon. In fact, it seems like it is only likely to grow.

Altogether, this first section has given us a brief history lesson and a slightly longer optimistic look at Servant Leadership. This is a good thing because, as we have seen, Servant Leadership is both valuable and positively impactful to organizations as a whole and employees individually.

But, despite all of this, I don't think that everything is "sunshine and cotton candy". I think there are some clouds on the horizon that need to be carefully addressed. And this is the topic of our next section!

# Section 2

## Where We Went Wrong

From everything we've looked at so far, one could walk away with the impression that Servant Leadership is pretty good as it is, and this book is just another swing at the same ball (pardon the baseball metaphor). But I'm sure that you know this isn't the case. I have already alluded to the idea that there is something amiss, and I plan to show how it can be improved. So, when is that going to start?

Well, before we could look at what went wrong, it was important that we understood the foundation that was laid, which took us down the path to where we are now. That is why we invested the first section into understanding the baseline of Servant Leadership and (hopefully) fairly describing the merit it possesses.

I want to take the next several short chapters looking at why it went from such a good idea to something that often entirely misses the mark of the heart and intent of Servant Leadership. The goal here is not to show that Servant Leadership is bad, per se. Rather, the intent is to show how it may have been unintentionally distracted from its purest intent. This will allow us to better understand how mindfulness improves the Servant Leadership model.

In this section, we will begin by affirming the fact that Servant Leadership, even in its current form, is not bad. In fact, it's even necessary. But we will also show how the necessary components of

Servant Leadership ruined its heart and why radical change is needed.

So, walk with me through the next few pages in which we will explore how such a good idea was (dare I say) corrupted by well-meaning people who simply let the messaging get a little off track and have facilitated a complete change in the motive of Servant Leadership.

# Chapter 5

## *Servant Leadership is Not Bad*

*"The best way to find yourself is to lose yourself in the service of others."*

— *Mahatma Gandhi*

If you picked up this book with the thought that I was going to share all the reasons Servant Leadership is bad, you were right. I'll share every bad thing about the philosophy of Servant Leadership right here.

Here are the top 3 reasons I think Servant Leadership is a problem.

1. Putting others first all the time can lead to exhaustion and self-neglect.

2. Too much support can create a culture where poor performance goes unchecked.

3. Some will exploit a servant-leader's kindness for their own gain.

What do you think?

No, you didn't get a bum copy of the book. And no, this is not a "Buy-my-premium-package-and-you'll-get-my-top-3-reasons. Servant Leadership-is-bad" pitch. The reality is: I don't think Servant Leadership has a problem.

I LOVE the idea that leaders are called to serve.

I love the idea that when leaders serve their team, the team tends to come together and serve one another.

I wish MORE leaders served by being empathetic to the situations their teams face.

I want everyone to grow. From the leader with the most responsibility to the most entry-level individual, growth should be something that is prioritized. Servant Leadership promotes that, and I agree!

I believe the ethical impact of Servant Leadership is something amazing as well! Shared decision-making results in less corruption, more synergy, and a better use of time, energy, and other resources!

Additionally, I will go to my grave sharing the value of empowerment! We even put out an entire series on the Servant-Minded Leadership YouTube Channel on the value of empowerment. Servant-leaders empower their team, and that is a wonderful thing that sets them up for success both in the short run and the long term.

> *"Servant-leaders empower their team, and that is a wonderful thing that sets them up for success both in the short run and the long term."*

I could go on and on about the benefits of Servant Leadership. The best leaders I have ever worked with and/or for have all been servant-leaders. You will read stories about some of them in the following pages, and I hope that you will be as inspired by reading about them as I was when I experienced them. I have worked diligently to be a servant leader, and I think, if you were to ask those whom I have had the privilege to lead, they would agree I gave it my best shot. (Whether I succeeded or not may be a different story!)

But let me tell you, it's not only a bunch of positive, feel-good vibes that make this work. There are tons of other benefits as well. The return on investment is pretty incredible. For example, just a few of the tangible benefits of the Servant Leadership paradigm are: higher client satisfaction, improved employee retention, fewer sick days, and greater productivity! These are also part of the package. When the leaders serve their teams well, the teams are empowered to serve the organization effectively, and the organization is enabled to serve the clients expertly. In the end, everyone is happy!

Yes, indeed, I think Servant Leadership is a fantastic idea, and I have no desire to tear it down!

# Chapter 6

## Servant Leadership is Necessary

*"Leadership is not about titles, positions, or flowcharts. It is about one life influencing another."*

— **John C. Maxwell**

We've established that Servant Leadership, as an idea, is pretty good. But I will take it a step further. I think that it's not only good, but it's also necessary. In fact, I submit for your consideration that Servant Leadership is necessary from multiple perspectives, including team dynamics, organizational productivity, financial considerations, and many more. Regardless of whether you are in HR, Finance, the executive suite, or an entry-level laborer, the idea of Servant Leadership is necessary to keep you happy.

What do I mean?

Great question! Let's look at this from five major perspectives of an organization: Executive, Finance, HR, Employees, and Management. As we go through each of these, I think it will be abundantly obvious that Servant Leadership is necessary for all of them to achieve their goals.

### Executive

Most executives, that I know, are concerned with one thing more than any other: Production. Whether this is more sales, more development, or more product, the key is always MORE! For the executive, things that help the organization produce more are good. Things that hinder/delay/mitigate production are NOT.

What does this have to do with Servant Leadership? Quite simply, the teams that are served and empowered well are more productive! They stay longer, take fewer sick days, and are overall happier. This all comes together to result in better results, something that is near and dear to the heart of every executive!

**Finance**

Do you happen to know how much it costs to replace staff? Obviously, there isn't one universally accurate number, but the average is a bit over $28,000! Even if you are not familiar with that statistic (or even if it isn't accurate in your industry), you are likely very aware of the idea that it costs less to keep a client than to obtain a new one. The same is true of your internal clients (staff). From downtime that impacts productivity (cue executive) to the cost of recruiters or hiring platforms, to interviews, drug tests, and background checks, to training and its inherent cost, a LOT goes into finding a new employee. This cost does not even consider the cost of potential lawsuits or theft that often occurs when an individual leaves due to poor leadership.

> *"The teams that are served and empowered well are more productive! They stay longer, take fewer sick days, and are overall happier."*

On the other hand, when there are solid leaders in place who know how to effectively engage with their staff, things tend to be done more efficiently, with less waste, while people remain committed to a job they love, in a company they feel connected to.

## Human Resources

A common frustration for most HR teams is the constant complaints they get about people's managers. From allegations of favoritism to complaints about ineffective communication, dealing with the challenge of ineffective leadership is the bane of most HR personnel.

This is not surprising. I read a statistic recently suggesting that 25% of people say they are currently working for the worst boss they've ever had. Needless to say, there is an intrinsic dissatisfaction with poor leadership, and it drains HR teams of their time, resources, and often leaves them disappointed when their mediation attempts are met with people continuing to walk out the door, leaving them to (once again) look for new people. (Have I mentioned that replacing people is expensive and hinders productivity?)

Thankfully, those organizations that have taken the time to invest in their leadership have found that people stay longer and spend more time working and less time complaining. I think of one company I worked with that experienced both a major increase in staff retention and a tremendous increase in recruitment results after they chose to begin investing in their front-line leaders. What a difference! And what a difference for HR!

## Employees

Obviously, the individuals who feel the most hurt from poor leadership are the people who are mistreated, confused, overworked, and unappreciated… While all of the previous entities and teams get most of the attention from leadership experts (after all, they are the ones who can pay for solutions), it is the employees of an organization who are really hurt by poor leadership. One study I read said that a direct supervisor has as much impact on a person's mental health as their spouse! It seems it goes without saying that if the leader is poor, the people they are leading are likely going to struggle!

Employees of poor leaders are not only individually hurt, but they tend to produce less and then complain before they leave. This leaves everyone we have spoken to with unmet expectations, frustration, and disappointment. And, it often extends to even more than the company, with individuals' home and community life being impacted as well.

But when employees have great leaders, the exact opposite is true. While the supervisor still has as much impact on the employee, it is positive, and that has amazing power for good in the world!

## Management

If you are thinking that poor leadership only impacts everyone besides the leader, that is not the case. In fact, most of the front-line leaders that I have met genuinely want to improve. They are simply ill-equipped to do so. What does this do? It creates leaders who are unsure of what to do. They understand their people are leaving, things are not getting done, and that HR is upset with them, but have no idea of how to fix it. Often, they are just as frustrated (albeit usually more silently) as everyone else.

They know that improving their leadership would make a huge impact, but they are unsure of how to do it, and so the frustration mounts as the problems pile on and everyone is upset. In general, there are few things that they would like more than to become an effective leader. If only they had the tools to do so. If only they knew HOW to be a servant-leader.

# Chapter 7

## *So, What's Wrong with Servant Leadership?*

*"The greatest danger in times of turbulence is not the turbulence; it is to act with yesterday's logic."*
— ***Peter Drucker***

We have invested a lot of time and words saying that Servant Leadership is good and necessary. So, what's wrong with it? From what we have said so far, it seems like there is no real issue. Of course, you know that can't be true, or we wouldn't be reading a book about the value of changing the Servant Leadership model. But, seriously. It all sounds pretty great so far, right? So, let's introduce how it has gotten off track.

Do you remember in the first section how we learned about the different people who have made Servant Leadership a household name? How do you think they did that? It certainly wasn't by them simply doing their jobs well and being great leaders. No! They went out and sold their theories! They provided workshops, seminars, and training. They wrote books. They gave speeches. They SOLD Servant Leadership.

Now, there is nothing wrong with being compensated for one's time. I certainly expect to be compensated for the value added by SML in the organizations we serve. But whenever there is a cost, there is an accompanying expectation. In the business world, it's called ROI— **"Return on Investment"**.

If, for any reason, you are not familiar with the idea of ROI, it can be summarized in this way: Any time an organization spends resources, there is a calculation of whether those resources were invested (used to grow the company) or wasted (showing no evidence of impact). The underlying idea is, if money is spent on something, it should be traceable to much MORE money coming in.

This may sound very clinical, but it really makes sense. After all, every company has a finite amount of resources. Of course, some have MUCH more than others, but none of them have an endless cash supply. Regardless of exactly what an organization has at its disposal, they are accountable for how they uses the resources they have. Whether it's shareholders, a board of directors, or simply the bank, businesses are beholden to someone for their finances. Therefore, they have to make decisions that serve the long-term financial interests of the organization well.

> *"It is not that there is any question in our minds about the value of Servant Leadership. But it is REALLY hard to demonstrate provable ROI on almost any training program."*

When organizations spend money on a seminar, workshop, speaker, or training system, there is a question that hangs heavy in the air. *How is this expense going to ultimately make us more money?* This is not only true when considering leadership development. This is ALWAYS the question. If there is an output, it must be "invested" and therefore, we need to know what the RETURN on that investment will be.

This reality has posed some level of challenge for purveyors of Servant Leadership offerings. It is not that there is any question in our minds about the value of Servant Leadership. But it is REALLY hard to demonstrate provable ROI on almost ANY training program.

I recall serving as the training manager for one organization. Every year, during my review time, there was always the same challenging question that my director and I faced. "How can we quantify 'success'?" Don't get me wrong. We KNEW that the training was valuable. We could see its impact. The culture was improving. The staff were doing better work. The clients were happier. But my scientist friends know that "correlation is not the same as causation". And proving causation is very difficult for any training or empowerment investment.

Because of the need to prove ROI, those who believe in Servant Leadership are faced with the unenviable task of showing WHY there should be an investment made into this leadership empowerment strategy. Whether it is the people selling the product or the people buying it, they all know that the ultimate question is, "What's the ROI going to be on this?"

When the question that is being asked all day is, "What about the ROI?" it can be REALLY tough to even think about "service" and/or "love"—even if they ARE core pillars of our offering. No, what has to be considered first and foremost is how this program is going to make us money. The reality is, organizations need to be able to point to wise stewardship of those resources.

I think of an organization that wanted me to provide coaching for several of their leaders. One of the things that they were fairly insistent upon was the measurables. They needed to be sure that the money they were spending was worth it. As we crafted a strategic plan for coaching their mid-level leaders, there was a single question that came up multiple times: "How are we going to hold them accountable to the goals that are identified?"

Eventually, I asked the C-suite, "Let me ask you a question: If they are not able to meet the stated objectives, are you prepared to release their talent to the market?" This question revealed the heart of what they were indirectly communicating. Their objective for wanting coaching was pure: they wanted to invest in the success of the leadership team. They knew it was the right thing to do, and they were willing to put in the work to do it. However, they wanted me to provide a guarantee of positive ROI, while they were not willing to deal with the inevitable results if the individual was led to water but would not drink.

The conversation allowed us to realign priorities. The goal was to invest in the people who were having a direct impact on the culture of the organization. Sure, if they were obstinate and refused to exhibit the qualities of a great leader (a desire to learn, grow, improve, etc.), then there would need to be an additional conversation. But how do you quantify the impact of a leader who knows how to effectively remediate? All that can be done is track things like employee turnover, client satisfaction, and other such things, and (over the long term) see if there are trends in a direction that is appreciated.

But this is the constant pull. While this is something that is intrinsically different between the messaging of Servant Leadership and Servant-*Minded* Leadership. (SML has a different focus than most.) They really struggled because every previous leadership company had come in promising the same basic measurable outcomes: increased revenue, decreased operating expenses, increased retention, etc. I wasn't talking about those things, even though it would have been honest to do so.

Why would I avoid these aspects of benefit to the organization, especially if I could do so with integrity? The reason is simple: *I believe that, while ROI is important, focusing on it is the single biggest problem with modern Servant Leadership.*

The idea of Servant Leadership can quickly be summed up in one sentence: "If you will serve your team, they will serve the mission (be more productive, achieve more, do more, create more, etc.)." This seems really good, on the surface. After all, it aligns with the much more recognized phrase, known as "The Golden Rule": "Do unto others as you would have them do unto you."

Over the years that I have been in various leadership circles, whenever the conversation of Servant Leadership (whether it's directly called that or not) is brought up, it always sounds about the same. "If you will do **'X'**, then your team will be more inclined to do 'Y'." And everyone nods, agrees, and offers their success stories about how this has worked for them.

Not only can most organizations point to increased employee retention, increased customer satisfaction, and increased productivity as a direct result of the implementation of Servant Leadership, but there are also numerous studies that support the idea that organizations that promote Servant Leadership will be more productive and see numerous other positive results.

Because of the results, both anecdotal and scientific, this form of leadership makes complete sense from a business perspective. Let's face it, business is business! There is one driving force that is more important than any other: Return on Investment (ROI). It is not that you don't care about your people, the environment, or your passion. But, if there is not SOME form of ROI, the business cannot sustain the output. In order to put time, energy, or money into an endeavor, the business has to be able to justify to itself that it will result in a greater return than output.

This is no more clearly seen than in the example of "charitable" sponsorships. Do organizations genuinely want to help their local t-ball team or Boys and Girls Club? Of course! Who wouldn't want to support the little sluggers as they round the bases? They absolutely DO want to provide support and enjoy investing in the lives of the next generation. But those who are familiar with fundraising recognize that the financial output cannot be sustained without some form of ROI. That is why the T-ball field is lined with the posters of the companies that have contributed, and why the Boys and Girls Club has sponsored art rooms. The reality of this community engagement and support is that there is an ROI factor that says, "I want to help, but I am going to need enough recognition to make my investment worth it. I am going to need my business to benefit in the process of helping you get new jerseys or paint supplies."

So, when we are discussing Servant Leadership, that is usually the conversation driver: "If you will serve your team, they will be more inclined to serve the mission." And by serving that mission, the organization will have greater productivity, larger margins, and greater overall success. As a part of this conversation, one may include that servant-leaders who serve their team usually facilitate higher morale, which improves overall attitude, ultimately facilitating significantly greater output on the part of the team and maybe even a promotion for you!

As an intrinsic communicator, I strongly believe in the power of words. The things that we say often influence, if not determine, our actions. Therefore, when all of our words reflect an emphasis on ROI, it becomes increasingly difficult to maintain any form of emphasis on being a true servant. This is the true challenge with Servant Leadership. And it may well have ruined it.

# Chapter 8

## *People, Progress, and Profit*

*"Treat your employees like they make a difference,*
*and they will."*

— **Jim Goodnight**

Have you ever heard the saying, "Our staff are our greatest asset?" If you were a member of that staff, did it make you feel good to know that your organization valued you and you weren't considered less important than the machinery? I hope so. I hope that you took those words and were encouraged that they didn't plan to replace you with a robot (yet). I hope that you were able to recognize that they wanted (if nothing else) for you to feel valued.

But, while I sincerely hope the idea was meaningful to you, I also know it was likely rooted in the same idea of ROI, previously discussed. It was based on the idea that, in order for an organization to do anything, it MUST have a proposed ROI. In this case, progress and profit for a company depend on its employees feeling valued and appreciated. If people don't feel appreciated, they quickly become discouraged and unmotivated, and the organization's productivity and profits sink. Therefore, for the benefit of the organization and its bottom line, there must be an effort made to ensure that employees feel appreciated and valued. Assets always result in an increase. (This is the quintessential difference between assets and liabilities: assets MAKE money and liabilities COST money.) Therefore, when an organization says that their staff are their greatest assets, what they are (at least) implying is that their employees provide the greatest ROI.

The idea is quite simple. Want happy employees? Show them you appreciate them. Want productive staff? Give them credit when they produce. Want motivated people? Share public recognition. You get the idea; if you want your staff to do good work and make you lots of money, you're going to have to at least throw them a bone once in a while. Why? Because profits and progress depend on employees feeling valued.

> *"Profits and progress depend on employees feeling valued."*

Even if you're not from the C-suite, it's pretty easy to see why this idea caught on. It was a no-brainer. The better an organization treats its employees, the better their employees will treat them, even if it's only because of their own perception of loyalty.

Interestingly, the idea didn't end there. Others began to take it further. People began to hear the WORDS of appreciation, but often they still did not FEEL appreciated—largely because words were not backed up with action. Because of this, many additional programs and ideas were introduced to the corporate world in order to address these issues. In Chapter 9, we'll look at how the idea of Servant Leadership progressed, and how there have been more and more efforts to make it better.

# Chapter 9

## Servant Leadership 2.0

*"The best way to predict the future is to create it."*
— *Peter Drucker*

Do you remember when you first heard about how major tech companies were treating their employees? Maybe you were one of the lucky ones who got to experience the glory days of Google, Facebook (now Meta), or some other tech start-up. Whether you got to experience it or simply heard about it from others, how did you feel when you heard about unlimited free food, drinks, and snacks provided in each department and nap pods? What about unlimited vacation and beer on tap? The perks these companies gave were extraordinary, and people were SUPER impressed! It sure beat the overpriced vending machines and stale coffee that most of us were stuck with!

Well, all of these ideas came from the same root: Servant Leadership. In this case, the implementation was simply answering the question, "How could the leadership team (executives, VPs, directors, etc.) serve the rest of the team?" Well, if a little bit of Servant Leadership was good, then even more would be better, right? Bring on the snacks, and let's grab a beer!

Treating employees well turned into even more great ideas as leadership development organizations began to abound and provide more ideas that leaders were encouraged to follow.

The idea that servant-leaders were called to stand in the point of conflict was an amazing concept that was added. This turned the idea of "(stuff) rolls downhill" and flipped it on its head. Once again, the truth was expressed. How will your staff remain motivated and productive if they are constantly trying to defend themselves and feel like they can do nothing right? They won't. Want to get the most from your staff? Then, leaders, you need to stand at the point of conflict. You need to be their advocate. You need to cover them and serve them in order to free them to do their best work.

> *"The blame is 100% for the leader, and the credit is for the team."*

Not only were leaders called to stand in the point of conflict, but they were also encouraged to take extreme ownership for the team. This meant that they owned the results, regardless of whether or not they had any direct involvement with a mistake or problem. Of course, don't forget, they were supposed to reflect credit back to the team. This meant that the blame was 100% for the leader, and the credit was for the team. This was another way that leaders were called to serve their team. Why? Because that is how you get the most from them. The team needed to know they were covered and that they could make mistakes. Otherwise, they were not going to be creative or proactive. That would mitigate productivity.

As these ideas took hold, people began saying things like, "Care about your staff as much as you want them to care about their work." This resulted in many policies, such as open-door times, employee engagement events, and wellness activities/retreats. The ROI was proven. Treat your staff well, and they will (usually) return the favor. If they don't, then try one of the other programs. That one is sure to work better.

Indeed, programs that promote some form of Servant Leadership have become increasingly common! A lot of companies have seen this trend as a cash cow and have begun selling their programs to other organizations. Everyone seems to have an idea of how to best engage with employees. Everyone wants to share their vision for how to maximize the impact of staff and how to get a great ROI from the employee-assets.

There is not a week that passes when I don't receive several emails from various organizations that are hosting webinars, sharing newsletters, soliciting participation, and ALWAYS trying to sell their solution for employee wellness, staff engagement, and leadership development.

The idea of serving the employees of an organization is a multi-trillion-dollar business, and it's not going away any time soon. I usually see a new company popping into my inbox about 1-2 times per month. Companies that want leadership consulting or cultural transformation or anything that falls into the employee-relations category have a plethora of options from which to choose, with more popping up every day!

Over the course of the past 60+ years, the idea of Servant Leadership has only grown. There are more programs, firms, and systems now than ever before, and there is no inclination to scale this back any time soon.

# Chapter 10

## Servant Leadership is Here to Stay

*"The function of leadership is to produce more leaders, not more followers."*

*— **Ralph Nader***

If you've been in the business world for more than a year or two, you've seen tons of programs, plans, policies, etc., arrive with great passion and momentum only to see those same ideas fall to the wayside after a relatively short period of time. I recall one place I worked that seemed to go through this cycle every 6-12 months. About that often, someone would come in with a big new idea and shake up the place. If we liked the idea, it was easy to get on board and hope it lasted. If we didn't like the plan, then it was easy to pretend to be on board, knowing that it wasn't likely to last more than 2-3 months. Then we could go back to the way it used to be.

I think it is safe to assume that my experience is not terribly unique. One person I knew used to say, "There is always policy, and there is always procedure, and they are rarely aligned." This is a direct result of what I described above. Someone implements a new idea, and that becomes the policy. But what actually happens long-term may or may not be aligned with the official directive.

In fact, it may be our own idea that falls by the wayside. It's not that we are not passionate about it. We just get tired of managing it.

So, we just let it ride. When we come back to the topic a year later, it becomes abundantly obvious that our grand plan did not stick, and the old drumbeat is still strong.

However, unlike the latest idea that you or your director just came up with, Servant Leadership is here to stay. If it was going to wear off or fall to the wayside, it would have done so already. Instead, over the course of the past 60 years, it has become deeply ingrained into the fabric of corporate life.

While there are certain pockets of those who still don't see the value (or who simply don't want to put in the work), for the most part, no successful organization openly rejects the idea of Servant Leadership. And, in the increasingly rare scenario that a leader doesn't at least pay lip service to the philosophy, they are pretty rapidly ousted. If they aren't replaced by their leadership, the employees will force them to change by walking out the door, leaving the dinosaurs to wonder what they could have done better. After all, they paid their staff every time, on time! What more do people want!?

> *"Servant Leadership is here to stay. If it was going to wear off or fall to the wayside, it would have done so already."*

This isn't to say that Servant Leadership is being perfectly implemented—or even that it's being implemented at all, for that matter. But you'll be hard-pressed to find someone who still thinks Servant Leadership is a fad. Even the leaders who are absolutely terrible at actually practicing the principles of Servant Leadership still give it lip service and often expect it from those who report to them.

People love the opportunity to feel like a good person and maybe even gain some kudos from their team. Nobody wants to be hated by their team and feel like they are the singular problem with a business. Servant Leadership provides a way for even the worst leaders to pretend to be the good guy. Even better, it gives truly great leaders a framework in which they can engage with their team.

Meanwhile, businesses appreciate the cultural implications of Servant Leadership, and they like the financial implications even more. They love the fact that the relatively small investment in coaching and other programs can save them billions of dollars a year in hiring, training, and legal costs. Plus, in certain cases, they also get to win "best-place-to-work" awards (or the like), and who doesn't love the free advertising that brings!? Because of these and a host of other reasons, many of which have been detailed in the previous chapters, there is little or no inclination or motivation to do away with Servant Leadership (hence the title of this chapter).

The fact that Servant Leadership is here to stay is good news for several reasons:

1. Servant Leadership is a good and positive method.
2. The ROI has been proven time and again.
3. Those providing the resources for the implementation of Servant Leadership will be happy to stay in business for the foreseeable future.

But, if I am saying that it's good… and that it is not going anywhere, why am I writing a book on how to fix it?

That's a GREAT question! We will address this important question in the next chapter.

# *Chapter 11*

## *What if the ROI is the Problem?*

*"The best leaders are those who are willing to serve first,
putting the needs of their team above their own."*
### *— Robert K. Greenleaf*

Have you ever had a **"friend"** ask you to help them move? The cheapest labor on the planet is friends helping friends move sofas, dressers, and other back-breakingly large objects in exchange for pizza, beer, and MAYBE the promise to return the favor in the future—the DISTANT future. When your friends called you to ask for help, I'll bet they didn't try to sell you on how amazing the pizza was going to be and how cold the beer would be.

Why not? Because the ROI was dismal. No one is going to think that it is a great deal to do 8-12 hours of manual labor in exchange for a $5 pizza and a couple of beers. (Never mind the fact that the full day of labor may have been described as just needing help with a couple of things that weren't very heavy, just awkward...) But what if your friend were a little more generous? What would it take for it to make sense to focus on the ROI? $50? $100? Maybe you are super **"selfish"** and wouldn't come for anything less than $500. If you are going to move things like a professional mover, you should be paid for it, right?

What would happen at that point? It would no longer be you helping a friend move. It just became a business transaction. You have agreed to stay until the job is done in exchange for $500. There is going to be less talking and joking and a whole lot more "put that over there."

Now, there's nothing wrong with someone paying for the help of their friends when moving day comes. But I can promise you that the minute it is a **"job"**, the fun goes right out the window, and the focus is the task at hand. It's actually kind of weird, right? I mean, who is a better friend, the one who wants you to break your back for a cheap meal, or the one who wants to pay you well to provide them with needed services? In theory, the one who is coughing up the cash is the better friend! And yet that's not how it works, is it? If you were paid $500 to help with moving, then there is no time for jokes or messing around.

This is EXACTLY what has occurred with Servant Leadership. The more organizations have spent on Servant Leadership programs and initiatives, the more the focus has become centered on the ROI. In fact, there is almost no emphasis at all on serving the team. It's all about the ROI. I challenge you to test this. Bring in ANY leadership consulting firm that promotes Servant Leadership. Ask them to tell you about what they do for businesses. Then, time how long it is before they mention money saved. I have found that it is usually less than 2 minutes into their pitch.

> *"The more organizations have spent on Servant Leadership programs and initiatives, the more the focus has become centered on the ROI... There is almost no emphasis at all on serving the team."*

Even ChatGPT is not immune to this reality. As a part of the same answer that provided us with the baseline for Servant Leadership in our introduction, the bot goes on to say, (emphasis mine);

*"This approach has been embraced in various fields and is considered a valuable way to promote **collaboration**, employee **engagement**, and **organizational success.**"*

Note that the goal is less about making an impact in the lives of those we are supposedly serving and more about promoting things that will result in more money and less turnover.

Again, it's not that the ROI is bad. The problem is that the ROI has become the focus. In our attempts to make things better, we have systematically made things worse. With every program that we buy and each coach we hire, our expectations of ROI increase. There is almost no emphasis on the SERVANT and an almost exclusive focus on the ROI.

I found a comment on one of my LinkedIn posts very insightful. With his permission, I quote Mark Wiggins, who said;

*"This is so true when you think about it, however, it has become obvious, the vast majority of so-called **'Leaders'** do not even have service in their vocabulary.*

*The very ideal of service has been lost in the miasma of self-help, winning the fight, and coming out on top books, and as often stated by Simon Sinek, there is no bookshop section titled **"Help Others"**!*

*As adults and as parents, we should understand that you learn from example, and you cannot ever expect anyone else to listen to you, if you ask them to do something you never have or never would do.*

*The ideal of service must be resurrected and understood to be why we are here, not to have others be of service to us, but to be of service to others without any thought ever about getting something in return."*

In my opinion, this is an incredibly accurate synopsis of the state of leadership today! We are doing all the stuff, but we are not actually serving. How can this be?

We hold open-door times for people to come and drop in, but do we actually care about them as they share?

We go out on the floor and connect with the staff, but do we genuinely desire to serve them?

We have more events, empowerment seminars, and employee engagement plans than we know what to do with, but do we actually see the employees we are pretending to serve as anything more than a position to fill?

When we implement a new Servant Leadership strategy, are we most concerned with positively impacting the lives of those on our team, or how much this is supposedly going to shave off the bottom line (or at least avoid adding to the budget)?

The problem is not with Servant Leadership. The problem is with the messaging around it. The problem is the way that it is presented, which has corrupted the way we think about it.

I am not immune to this phenomenon. I actually have three separate pitches that I use to promote the services of SML Consultive. One is for HR Leaders. It focuses on the ROI of employee retention and client satisfaction. The second is for Executives. It focuses on Client satisfaction and the COST of bringing on new staff to replace the staff that the leaders have run off. And the third pitch is for leaders themselves. This one focuses on the true idea of Servant Leadership and emphasizes the unique opportunity of leaders to positively impact the lives of those they lead.

While we will talk MUCH more about how to make what is contained in my third pitch the emphasis on leadership development, the reality is we ALL are faced with the reality that if there is no benefit to the overall organization, then there is no reason for them to spend precious resources like time or money on the service.

So, if we are somewhat stuck in the rut of having to share how there is an ROI—and yet that is precisely what is ruining the concept of Servant Leadership—what is to be done? Decisive and impactful action must be taken, post haste!

# Section 2

## *Conclusion*

After taking time to revel in the history of Servant Leadership in Section 1, we invested the last several chapters into what went wrong.

The emphasis on ROI wasn't intentional. There was no malice. In fact, some may even say that the problem I have described is more semantical than actual. Yet, it is there. There is an underlying transactional current in the conversation of Servant Leadership. While leaders are called to be in the business of empowerment, inspiration, and transformation, an unfortunate undertow of transnationalism can cause us to lose our footing and be swept away in the tide of ROI.

Unfortunately, with more proponents of Servant Leadership, the problem became even more challenging, as the narrative became more about the ROI than the true opportunity of leaders to serve. What should have been a great boon to the idea of Servant Leadership has become its greatest demise. This is why it became necessary for there to be a solution—another option—that allows the focus to shift and return to the noble cause upon which it once rested.

That is the topic of our next section! Let me introduce you to Servant-MINDED Leadership!

# Section 3

## *How Mindfulness Changes Servant Leadership*

Vivian came to the US from Spain. And while she took to the English language very quickly, she often used words that were very close to correct or were even a direct translation from her native tongue, but their connotation did not work for her intended American English use. She might say something like, "I will check the mail until 5 o'clock." Now, what she meant was that she intended to go check the mail at 5. (Or literally, she would not be checking until 5). But, by her wording, one could easily arrive at the conclusion that she intended to stand by her mailbox until 5.

Despite using the wrong word, people often understood what Vivian intended to communicate because her word choice forced them to ask questions. It stood out of place just enough that they would stop and think about her statement and ask for clarification. This would allow for dialogue to occur and a better understanding.

We invested the first two sections of this book looking at where Servant Leadership comes from and what it has come to. We have explored the benefits, the selling points, and the value that it brings. We have also discussed the downfall its messaging has brought and recognized its impact is being mitigated by well-intentioned people who have the burden of justifying the cost of their worthwhile products.

In this section, we will see why a change in semantics like adding the word **"minded"** significantly impacts the value of such a noble concept. Now, you may be thinking, "Jon, just because you added the word 'minded' to the phrase, doesn't change anything." And, in a sense, I completely agree with you. But I would contest that, in another sense, a simple word changes everything!

Just like Vivian's word choice stood out to her listeners and often resulted in questions about meaning, I think adding a word like "minded" does the same for the worn-out phrase "Servant Leadership." This gives one the opportunity to share the differences and may even result in someone assessing whether they truly believe in Servant-Minded Leadership or if they are more interested in the ROI.

The reality is, there is great power in words. Words not only convey meaning, but they also assign meaning based on our perceptions. When we tear down the usual boundaries of understanding, it opens the opportunity for more. In other words, when something doesn't nicely fit into the mental norms that we have established, it results in us giving it a second thought.

That is one of the things that adding the word **"minded"** to **"Servant Leadership"** does. It causes people to stop and say, "Wait, what? What do you mean by that?" This can create space to be present and engage with what it means to truly have a servant's heart.

In this third section, we will explore what it means to add the word **"minded"** to the Servant Leadership dynamic, and how it results in leaders who are more servant-minded as well as organizations that are more interested in true leadership development.

# *Chapter 12*

### *What is Leadership Mindfulness?*

*"To handle yourself, use your head; to handle others, use your heart."*

— **Eleanor Roosevelt**

The Oxford Dictionary defines "mindful" as *"conscious or aware of something."* When we use the phrase "Servant-Minded Leadership," we are promoting the idea of mindfulness in regard to Servant Leadership. We want to be conscious or aware of the concepts that make up Servant Leadership. This is in contrast to the consciousness or awareness that usually surrounds Servant Leadership: namely, Return on Investment (ROI).

Adding the word "minded" encourages us to ask ourselves what we mean, and what Servant Leadership actually is. Mindfulness is the active engagement with the concept of Servant Leadership. It calls us to perceive and engage with the topic in a certain way, and by default, NOT engage in other ways.

For example, Servant-MINDED Leadership is NOT a "program." I am often asked about my program; everyone seems to want a program. The problem with programs is that they are largely ineffective. Let's be honest: you and I are unique! We do not have

57

the exact same strengths or weaknesses. No "program" is going to impact us both in the same. In fact, the more widely applicable a program is, the less dynamically impactful it will be. So, no, I do not have a "program". I have a method that we use to empower leaders individually to operate in the concepts of Servant-Minded Leadership. But I do not offer a single "program".

Since it is not a program, it is also NOT a quick-fix solution. Many organizations that have been sold on the idea of ROI think that someone can come in, offer their solution (program), and soon thereafter, all their problems are going to be fixed. This is disappointing because no one can actually deliver these types of results, at least not in mass. Might a few people have an epiphany at one of my events? Well, I certainly hope so! But systemic change does not happen overnight!

> *"Expecting Servant Leadership to provide a quick-fix to problems that have probably been developing for many years is like expecting a single dose of vitamins will cure someone of high blood pressure."*

Expecting Servant Leadership to provide a quick fix to problems that have probably been developing for many years is like expecting a single dose of vitamins will cure someone of high blood pressure. No one would expect that. What takes years to build can take even longer than that to undo and improve. When it comes to our physical health, we recognize that if we have not been loving our bodies, we are going to have to give them some TLC for a good amount of time in order to bring them into a place of optimal performance.

So, if it is not a quick-fix program, what IS Servant-Minded Leadership?

First, Servant-Minded Leadership is an authentic love for others. As sappy as that may sound, it is truly the heart of Servant-Minded Leadership. In fact, this is the root of true Servant Leadership. As we are mindful of where we have been placed and the opportunities that lie before us, we begin to intentionally love others.

This is a somewhat radical idea. It is not new, but it is radical. Let me give you an example. One day, I posted this image on LinkedIn:

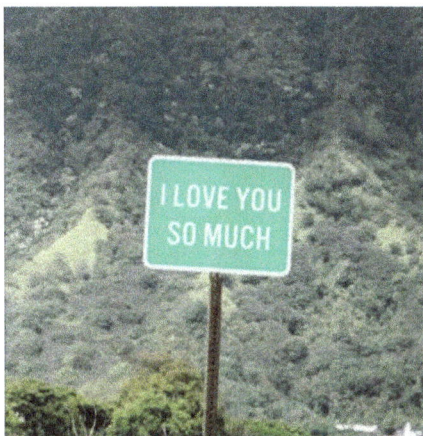

I then asked the question:

*"Leaders, if you sent this to your team, what would they think? Would this be odd, or would they see it as something that aligns with the way you engage with them on a daily basis?"*

While I knew the question would generate some conversation and maybe even some controversy, I was somewhat disappointed when one leadership coach commented:

> 1y ⋯
>
> If you sent this sign without context to see what people would say, you might find yourself being investigated for sexual harassment. It is sad, but frankly, that is where we are in the business realm.
>
> Like | Reply · 2 replies

Now, whether this person is right or wrong is not the point. After all, context certainly is key to ALL communication. The real question I feel needs to be answered is: Do we authentically love our teams enough in our day-to-day interactions that a message like this would be properly understood?

I don't always respond to comments—especially those that may be designed JUST to incite emotion but I chose to engage this one by saying:

**Jon Antonucci** Author · 1y · ···
Servant-Minded Leader | Growth Love...

Indeed! That is precisely the point of the post, ███████████████.
The context of our everyday interactions (including our regular communication patterns) will either result in this being taken as an authentic expression of genuine care and empowerment or it will be an unusual communication that results in suspicion and (as you mentioned) quite possibly a negative impression.

I know of many, many people who like to throw the L-word around. They love everything and everyone. Unfortunately, their words and actions are not aligned. If they sent their team this sign, it would be met with suspicion.

Here is a real-life example that I saw posted by one of my acquaintances:

Take a look at the screenshot of their conversation.

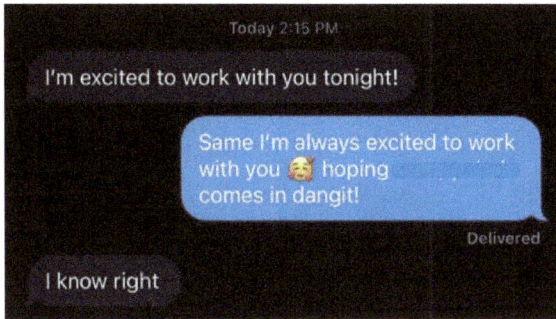

At first glance, it looks like a perfectly reasonable conversation, maybe even reciprocal! But here is the post that accompanied it:

> *"What is my manager trying to butter me up for? 😊 I do like working with her lol but why is she sayin that to me. People don't say nice things like that to me. It's suss 😊😊😵"*

What a terrible paradigm! This leader (presumably) was trying to motivate, encourage, and inspire their staff. Yet, presumably because there was no pattern of love and respect, their text message was received with suspicion and reposted on social media in the context of suspicion for all of the world to see. I happen to know that this particular person ultimately quit specifically due to what she described as a "bi-polar manager."

Of course, we could dissect whether the recipient was projecting or engaging any number of other factors all day long. But I really want to stay focused on the leadership capacity revealed in these examples.

The Servant-Minded Leader has an authentic love for people in general, and that is manifested easily via their interactions with their team. They do not have to manufacture love that comes across as odd because it is a daily experience. And that brings us to the second thing that I would say that Servant-Minded Leadership actually is.

61

Servant-Minded Leadership is the genuine desire to facilitate the best for your team. While the messaging of Servant Leadership has been centered around what one can get FROM their team, Servant-MINDED Leadership is focused on what one can get FOR their team. This is not an us-vs.-them perspective. We are not trying to get something from the organization on behalf of our team at least not all the time. But we should be most interested in how we can serve them.

The authentic desire for what is best for the team is also called love. Servant-Minded Leadership is rooted in authentic love for people. Because of our love for our team, we want what is best for them. This is true in any relationship. True love wants what is best for the other person. This also applies to working relationships.

But wanting and even working for the best for another person does not mean that we give them everything that they want. There are many things that I have hoped for and desired in life that were NOT what was best for me. I am pretty sure all I have to do is go back to last night's dinner at the Cheesecake Factory and realize that wanting to start by ordering from the dessert case was not what was best for me. Just like I required myself to eat a nutritious meal before indulging in a slice of fresh banana cream cheesecake, so I would require certain things from my team that are what is best for them.

We will cover this more later, in the book, but it is important that we do not confuse love with enablement. Loving them means to want and do what is best, not necessarily what is desired.

Third, as a part of having an authentic love for others, the Servant-Minded Leader has a sincere desire to fulfill their position with excellence. This means that they are not looking for shortcuts, nor are they trying to do as little as possible. Like me, you may have had a boss who spent more time taking credit for your work than doing any actual work themselves. This is the antithesis of a Servant-Minded Leader.

Excellent execution is important to the Servant-Minded Leader. They want to do everything at the highest level. They expect as much (or more) from themselves as they do from their team. This leader can be easily identified from their willingness to assist wherever needed. They do not know the words "That's not my job" while simultaneously being experts at true delegation and empowerment.

In fact, even when the Servant-Minded Leader decides that it is in the best interest of all to hand off certain responsibilities, they do so with excellence. They are not inclined to simply rid themselves of the items they don't want to do. Instead, they delegate the matters that are most effectively handled by others, and they align the assignments with the capability to execute at the highest level.

Additionally, because love has a trust component, the Servant-Minded Leader understands that, when it is time to delegate something, they must give BOTH the responsibility AND the authority, within supportive boundaries. In other words, the individual must be empowered to provide authentic input if they are to be held responsible for the output.

So, what is Leadership mindfulness?

Well, what it's NOT is a program or a quick fix. No matter how attractive these types of "solutions" are, they are not actually effective, and Servant-Minded Leadership does not claim these attributes. Instead, the Servant-Minded Leader has an authentic love for others and seeks to both exude and empower excellence at every level.

In the next couple of chapters, we will look at some of the things that one can do on the path toward Servant-Minded Leadership.

# *Chapter 13*

## *Question Everything*

*"To be a leader, you must be a servant first."*
— ***Robert K. Greenleaf***

When a child is very young, they tend to ask the same question over and over and over… and over.

**Mom:** *"Pick up your toys!"*
**Child:** *"Why?"*
**Dad:** *"That is a tree."*
**Child:** *"Why?"*
**Parent:** *"I love you!"*
**Child:** *"Why?"*

Despite being sometimes aggravating to parents, in reality, this is a critical part of a child's growth process. It is an important mechanism that tends to wane over time, as the child feels that such questions are an imposition instead of a welcome inquiry. By the time we are in positions of leadership, we are not at all inclined to ask why. And yet, it is critical that we do!

Among the questions that I suggest we should ask are:

- "Why am I here?"
- "What is my purpose?"
- "How can I make a difference?"

If you are thinking, "Gee, Jon, this is getting pretty deep for a leadership book!" I don't blame you. But I DO think that these are REALLY great questions to ask ourselves, albeit maybe not as deep as they originally appear.

Before I share what I'm specifically talking about, let me just say that if you have never engaged these questions on a personal level, I STRONGLY encourage you to do so before you attempt to answer them in the context of your business or leadership position. Go on a three-day solo retreat and wrestle with these ideas. Seriously, get rid of your computer, phone, and any other distractions. Then go to a secluded place and ponder your existence. You may think that you don't have time for such exercises, but I would say that you don't have time NOT to. Better to invest a weekend into clarity and purpose than to waste your life with a lack of direction.

> *"Better to invest a weekend into clarity and purpose than to waste your life with a lack of direction."*

Once you have general/overall clarity, then it is time to apply these questions to our position of leadership. If we are to be Servant-MINDED Leaders, then we must have the presence of mind to engage with questions such as these.

*Why am I here?*

Wouldn't it be great if all leaders could move forward with the knowledge and assurance that we were placed in our positions because we were the best person for the job and we would be delegated all the necessary authority so we could really make a dynamic impact? Unfortunately, that is not always the case, is it?

Often, leaders are placed in positions of leadership because they are:

- The technical expert.
- The longest tenured member of a team.
- The next person up.
- Expected to address a **"problem"**.
- Needed to meet a staffing quota.
  Etc.

Honestly asking ourselves why we are in a place can have a dynamic role in helping us to be effective leaders. As we are mindful about both the explicit reasons for our placement as well as the implied ones, we can determine how we can best serve our team.

### *What is my purpose?*

Closely aligned with the first question, this second one asks what is expected of us. Mindful consideration of what is expected of us and what our purpose is in that position will allow us to effectively engage with the staff via clear communication and consistent expectations. This will, of course, in turn, allow them the same luxury of understanding the purpose of their roles and how they fit into the overall whole.

### *How can I make a difference?*

The Servant-Minded Leader recognizes that their role does not end with their job description. Beyond the expectations of the organization, they have high expectations for themselves. In fact, it could be effectively argued that this is the quintessential difference between Servant Leadership and Servant-Minded Leadership. While Servant Leadership asks, "What can I do to get the most from my team?" The Servant-Minded Leader asks, "How can I make the biggest impact in the lives of those I'm leading?"

This question (assuming it's answered productively) may just be the single biggest catalyst toward being the embodiment of what a Servant-Minded Leader is.

These are not the only questions that we should be asking. But they are certainly a good start. They allow us to have a foundation of mindfulness that facilitates both introspection and impact. You may have an entirely different or additional list of questions that you are asking as a leader, and that is great!

The key is that we are asking questions. Too often, that curious child within has been so mercilessly beaten down that the LAST thing we do is ask questions. We fear looking silly or as if we don't know something we are supposed to know (more on this in the next chapter). Whether we are asking questions centered around our purpose in our position, or we are asking questions about our staff and what is meaningful to them, or we are asking questions about why the team functions as it does, we should be asking questions.

When I was about seven, I walked over to the next-door neighbor's house and said, *"I'm sorry to bother you, but I have a question."* The neighbor looked me square in my 7-year-old eyes and said, **"You don't need to be sorry for asking a question; that's the way we learn."** It's been a few decades now, and that interaction still resonates with me. (Thank you, Mr. McKinley.)

The reality of life is, if we are not growing, we are dying. From a human perspective, if we are not learning, we are dying. And, as my wise neighbor told me at seven years old, asking questions is how we learn! Of course, I have now come to understand that we can learn in all sorts of ways, but asking questions is certainly one of them.

So, if we want to make an impact, we have to ask questions… LOTS of questions! This will help us to avoid many of the traps of leadership—even Servant Leadership, which may be the way we've always done it. It will also facilitate a level of mindfulness that will improve the way we lead and the way we do business. And, if we get into the habit of asking lots of questions, it will make our next step much easier!

# Chapter 14

## I Don't Know What I Don't Know

*"The mind is like a parachute. It doesn't work if it isn't open."*
— *Frank Zappa*

I once had a roommate who was an investigative reporter for a local newspaper. One day, he told me that one of the foundational rules of journalism was "Always get a second source." If you have a tip, don't take their word for it check it out. If you have a story, always corroborate the details with multiple people. And, if your mother tells you that she loves you, be sure to get a second source!

This obvious tongue-in-cheek journalism emphasized the value of asking questions and not believing the first thing that we hear. This can be hard, especially for the servant-leader. Why? Because we may think that Servant Leadership and empathy mean we treat everyone as if they are right. Unfortunately, the reality is, they rarely are.

Just recently, I was speaking with a business coach who shared a story of a client who was trying to be a great leader: a leader of empathy and compassion. This leader actually gave their staff everything they asked for... and couldn't figure out why it still wasn't enough. This coach had to share with their client that sometimes there are times when "No" is the most loving thing we can say.

This doesn't mean that we have to be overly blunt or harsh. What it means is that we recognize at all times that there is probably more to the story.

You see, no matter how much the person we are listening to is TRYING to fairly represent a situation, they are probably not doing so in an unbiased manner. While we should certainly listen, understand, and authentically empathize with them, we should also recognize that we all have inherent biases, and we will serve them (both the person and the overall team) better to listen with the intent to understand and then follow that with additional research and listening. Then, an effort must be made to verify any conclusions that are reached.

> *"The Servant-Minded Leader takes time to be present in the situation while simultaneously evaluating the bigger picture and recognizing the humanity of those that they lead."*

The Servant-Minded Leader is not trying to "check a box" of Servant Leadership. If they were, they would listen, take what is said seriously, and take action. While this is admittedly better than what often happens, it is not necessarily the best way to handle it.

The Servant-Minded Leader takes time to be present in the situation while simultaneously evaluating the bigger picture and recognizing the humanity of those that they lead. Giving dignity is of utmost importance. And this means that the bigger picture is thoughtfully considered and the person before us is held in the same regard as others who are also a part of the team.

That last paragraph seems a bit philosophical, doesn't it? Let me try to provide a bit more clarity. If one has been a leader for very long, they have probably had an employee ask for a raise. This is very natural, and if the person has increased the value they add to the team, it is best to work with them to help them meet their goals.

But, while I support generous compensation, there is a reality that must be faced: if a raise were given every time it was requested, the company would soon go bankrupt. Therefore, it is imperative to balance the servant aspect (try to give employees as much as possible) with the mindfulness of recognizing that there is a bigger picture to be maintained. Sure, we all want a raise, but more than a raise, most of us want consistent employment. Therefore, the best way to be servant-minded is to balance what is right and fair with what is authentically feasible.

This is why mindfulness is so important. Servant Leadership, as good as it is, can be short-sighted. But if we are a Servant-Minded Leader, we will have the opportunity to make a dynamic impact over a longer period. The above example is just an easy one. The same principle applies to every aspect of leadership. Here are a few more examples of how mindfulness might apply to our everyday work:

- Obtain the perspective of multiple people before making a decision. (Don't believe everything the first person tells you [or act/decide on it].)
- Think about the overall picture when approving family/vacation time. (The interests of the individual must be mitigated by the interests of the whole.)
- Assume that there are details you aren't aware of. (Remember, you don't know what you don't know.)

Every leader will face the challenge of wanting to make immediate decisions without knowing all the facts. The old-school leader may make these decisions based on how they are feeling at the moment. The Servant Leader may take action based on how the employee in front of them is feeling at the moment. But the Servant-Minded Leader recognizes that they don't know what they don't know and, therefore, there are almost always more questions to be asked, and there is almost always more perspective to be gained.

This allows them to effectively serve their team and to be able to do so over the long term.

When we add mindfulness to the Servant Leadership dynamic, we begin to understand a critical truth: *I don't know what I don't know!* While servant-leaders have a desire to serve others, too often we think that the best way to serve them is to tell them what (we think) we know. Of course, most leadership books will tell you to listen. Many will even tell you to be sure to listen to understand. But how many emphasize that we don't actually know nearly as much as we think we do? The Servant-Minded Leader has a genuine desire to understand and recognize that even what IS known is not all there is to know.

# Chapter 15

## My Way or the Highway to the Byway

*"The best way to predict the future is to create it."*
— *Peter Drucker*

Over the course of my life, I have been privileged to serve under some GREAT leaders. My clients and I still benefit from the wisdom and practical disciplines that I witnessed in their leadership and lives.

I recall a conversation with one such leader as we were discussing a meeting he'd just led. He and I shared a pre-meeting, and I knew what his intentions were for the general meeting. But when it began, it seemed like he had abandoned his original plan, which I thought was far superior to the one he had ultimately agreed to. As I tried to share why I thought his original plan was better and attempted to convince him that we should revert to it, he said something that challenged my frame of thinking and forever changed the way that I lead.

He told me that many years ago, he'd learned that letting people do things their way was often more productive than asking them to do it his way. He further explained that the passion and dedication that people possess when engaging in a project or situation with their own solution is often significantly more successful than if they had been forced to implement his "better" way.

This was revolutionary to me. I had always approached leadership from the Servant Leadership approach of empowerment and elevation. I thought that, as a leader, it was my job to provide my team with the best tools to do the best work. Often, I interpreted this to mean that if I was the most knowledgeable or had the most experience in the room, I should give them the information for how to do it "right" and then commission them to work within the bounds of the paradigm I had set.

I was thoroughly challenged by the idea that letting people do it **"wrong"** could actually be MORE positively impactful and empowering. The mindfulness of empathy and true delegation completely shattered my "help-them-do-it-right" mentality. It reminded me of a time when my wife was in a car accident. Now, I am the furthest thing from a grease monkey, and when I saw the front of her 1999 Ford Explorer mangled with the radiator

> *"I was thoroughly challenged by the idea that letting people do it 'wrong' could actually be MORE positively impactful and empowering."*

leaking out the bottom, my "solution" was to get a new vehicle. She was not so quick to accept my solution. Being a bit more "blue-collar" than I am (she is a specialty TIG welder in the aerospace industry), she decided that she wanted to fix her own car!

I could have pushed back. I could have argued. But I knew better. If she wanted to fix it, I had to at least let her try. And guess what? She did it! She and her father worked on it for a few weekends, and instead of spending tens of thousands of dollars on a new vehicle for her, she had it fixed and operational within a few weeks for under $3k. Plus, she got to enjoy some quality father-daughter time, which I know meant the world to both of them.

There are multiple leadership lessons in this one story, but notice how my "better" way was not the BEST way. Note how empowered my wife was to fix it herself something that she enjoyed MUCH more than either one of us would have had if we had gone car shopping! Is her truck perfectly restored? No. Would a new vehicle have been nicer? Yes. But would it have been right to insist that we get a new vehicle? Not even a little bit! It would have been tragic for me to insist on my **"right"** way. Not only would it have cost more, but it would also have destroyed morale and would have given less ownership and, thus, pride in a job well done.

This was a terribly difficult lesson to learn. And honestly, I'm not sure I've mastered it yet. But it is a worthwhile principle for me to pass along. It very well could be the single greatest leadership hack I can give you.

Think about it: What is more servant-minded than facilitating a work environment in which people are empowered to step into their passions and execute the job in the best way they can? When we tell someone how to do something, we may think that we are "serving" them. But most of the time, we are simply serving ourselves: our timeline, our agenda, our reputation, our ego, etc.

Now, this story might seem somewhat silly. After all, is there really a parallel between my wife's car accident and leadership in an organization? I say yes! In fact, I believe that this is actually just the tip of the iceberg of a problem that most leaders have: a general attitude of "my way or the highway" attitude. This can manifest in various ways. Here are the levels of this phenomenon, as I see them:

- "Around here, it is my way or the highway!"
- "I'm the boss, and I said to do it this way…"
- "I was chosen to be responsible for this project, and I want to make sure it is done correctly; therefore, you need to do it this way."

- "I just want us to do the best work, and I have a lot of experience in this, so why don't you go ahead and do it the way I told you?"
- "As the leader, it is my job to set you up for success, so I have gone ahead and written out exactly how to do this so that we succeed."
- "You can do it however you would like, but THIS is the way that I would do it if I were you!"

Some of the above lines are nuanced. And I am sure that the argument can be made that some of them are legitimate ways to lead. But, overall, the issue is that these statements tend to reflect a heart that is thoroughly convinced that we know the best way and everyone else (or at least everyone on our team) is wrong (or at least not as good). This is not Servant-Minded Leadership, nor is it productive.

The minute that we genuinely think we have all of the answers is the minute that we cease to effectively lead. Why? Because a cup that is already full cannot be filled. Because the one who already knows cannot be taught. Because the leader who thinks they know all they need lacks humility and empathy.

Does this mean that we never provide advice and never share our experiences? NO! Of course not! It doesn't even mean that there are never times when it is 100% appropriate to say, "We WILL do it this way, or we will be removing people from the team!" But it DOES mean that we should never see ourselves as superior to others, and our minds should always be open to alternative ideas, solutions, and ways of doing things.

So, what is the opposite? How do we apply this in a positive way? The Servant-Minded Leader sees the members of their team as unique contributors and dynamic collaborators. They recognize that there may be more than one way to accomplish something. Furthermore, they understand that ways which are different (and even seemingly inferior) to their own are not "wrong". They see the value in diversity and cherish the contribution of each variance.

In the heart of the Servant-Minded Leader, "My way or the highway" goes to the byway.

# Chapter 16

## Proper Nouns

*"The most important thing in communication is hearing what isn't said."*

— **Peter Drucker**

What a strange title for this chapter, right? Why would I call it "Proper Nouns"? It's not as weird as it seems. But to understand it, we have to go on a bit of a trip down memory lane. Do you remember your elementary school days? If you do, you may recall that there is a difference between a "noun" and a "proper noun". Do you remember what it is?

**Noun** – *A general person, place, or thing.*

**Proper Noun** – *A specific name of an entity.*

"Ok, Jon… yeah, that's great," you say, "but you still haven't explained why you would name a chapter 'Proper Nouns'."

Ahhh… you got me. I haven't. But it IS intentional. That I can promise you! Here is why the chapter is named as it is: Your team is made up of PROPER NOUNS—not just nouns.

Sometimes, leaders think that their position requires them to remain aloof and to speak of and act toward their team as if they are objects. We have all heard the saying, "I ain't nothing but a number to them." This popular phrase well illustrates the feeling that many workers have had about the way their boss thought of them. In fact, it's likely you have felt that way at some point in your career.

Servant-Minded Leaders recognize not only that there are things they do not know and there are other ways of doing things, but also that the people who are on the team are valuable as unique individuals. In this way, the Servant-Minded Leader seeks to actually know their people, not just *about* them.

To be perfectly clear, I am in no way, shape, or form suggesting that the relationship between a leader and their staff should be anything other than appropriate and professional. However, "professional" does not have to mean aloof and certainly should not be cold. The Servant-Minded Leader is one who has a genuine love for their team and who authentically cares for them. It is impossible to effectively reach team members in a personal way if the leader does not take time to truly get to know them.

> *"The Servant-Minded Leader seeks to actually know their people, not just about them."*

This may include simple measures like asking good questions, paying attention when they are speaking, and making notes of important aspects of their life. This is a practical chapter as we explore how to live this principle out in day-to-day life.

Asking good questions shows that we care. This should NOT be an interrogation, nor should it be more personal than the individual is comfortable with. In fact, good questions should always make the person feel MORE comfortable and thoroughly cared for.

I recognize this is an uncomfortable suggestion for many leaders. Often, the only time we are accustomed to asking questions is when we are checking on work or when we are ensuring that we are ready to pass inspection. Trying to ask meaningful questions that are both genuinely personal while simultaneously not awkward can pose quite a challenge.

I will admit that it will probably take some practice. I am still practicing the art of asking good questions! But, while the first several conversations are likely to feel stilted and strange, over time they will become more comfortable. And, as you consistently engage with your people, they will realize that your heart to know them as individuals is genuine, and the awkwardness will seem like nothing more than a step on the journey of love.

Unfortunately, as challenging as it is to ask good questions, that is not all there is to this art of recognizing the individual people on our team. We also have to genuinely listen when they are answering!

The simple reality for those in leadership roles is that we have a LOT to think about. Most of us are multitaskers, and few of us are truly present in the moment when we are in conversation with our team. But the Servant-Minded Leader seeks to know people, and this is facilitated by taking a genuine interest in what they have to say. The leader who cares is the leader who listens. The leader who listens is the leader who knows their people.

The chances are good that, if you have been in leadership for very long, you have taken an "Active Listening" course of some sort (or are at least familiar with the concept). These are the lessons that encourage us to nod sympathetically, rehearse and repeat what is said, and use statements like, "What I hear you saying is _____, is that correct?" While all of these strategies of active listening are good and have their own benefit, none of them are a good replacement for authentically paying attention to our people.

I can manufacture "active listening". In fact, if I am honest, I have done so! I can nod based on your tone, participate with platitudes, and even rehearse general concepts about what you have said, all while my mind is 100 miles away thinking about 1,000 different things. None of this is paying attention.

But this is where things get tricky. The reality is, rehearsing with one's own words is a great strategy to remember what is said. And nodding empathetically can be a great communication tool. So, please do not think that I am suggesting that we avoid these tactics. What I am saying is that they are not good enough on their own. The key to a good strategy is a proper heart.

The heart of a Servant-Minded Leader is one that genuinely desires to know and understand their people. The nodding is not so that people will THINK they are being heard, it is the outpouring of one who is authentically engaged. The rehearsal of the concept is not a mechanism for holding the conversation. It is a measure to ensure effective understanding and hopefully the ability to remember the concepts discussed.

In short, we care! We see our people as valuable and worthy of dignity. And in that place, we actually want to listen, understand, and even remember!

If we are truly listening, we will be able to easily take part in the third step: take note of important things in their life. Did they mention that their dog just had puppies? It would mean the world to them if you asked about the puppies in your next conversation! Did they mention a sick child? How meaningful would it be to send a get-well-soon card? Did they share that Christmas is tough because it is the time of year in which a loved one died? Making note of such a comment and acting appropriately later demonstrates a true Servant-Minded Leadership approach!

This is commonly referred to as "follow-up", but it is rarely thought of in these terms. Follow-up conversations are often engaged when working on a project, in the midst of delegation, or even when there are remediation measures in place. But rarely do most bosses circle back to ask about the sick mother or check on the housing situation. This is a travesty!

Part of seeing our people as unique is getting to know their distinctives. This is only effective if we actually recall them and then circle back. Something as small as making a note of and acknowledging an individual's birthday can mean the world to them, especially when it comes from their leader!

In one organization that I worked with, they had an employee dashboard. On that portal, there was a "Celebrate" page, where people's birthdays and work anniversaries were listed. It was accurate and very easy to access. Therefore, I was astonished at how few of the upper-level leaders took the time to check it and offer a note of congratulations or well-wishes.

You may not have a nifty dashboard that tells you every birthday, but you can make a note of them as you find out. You may even be able to reach out to your HR department and ask for a list of all birthdays so that you can celebrate them. But again, the point is NOT to check a box by sending a card. The goal is to thoughtfully engage with your team in a way that communicates your heart for them, which I hope is one of love, care, and admiration!

# *Section 3*

## *Conclusion*

The idea of Servant-Minded Leadership is wrapped up in the idea of mindfulness, being the active engagement with the concept of Servant Leadership. It's not a **"Program"**. It is not a quick fix. It's a desire to fulfill the responsibility that we have been given with a spirit of excellence. Simultaneously, it is an authentic love for others. How does Servant-Minded Leadership embody these characteristics?

First, mindfulness asks questions in order to understand why one is in a position of leadership. It desires to understand the purpose of being in a position of leadership and seeks to discern how the most dynamic impact can be made.

Then, the Servant-Minded Leader recognizes that they do not know everything, yet they don't know what they don't know. Therefore, they are open to the ideas of others and believe that their way is not THE way. Then, as they are open to the input and ideas of others, they seek to know the people they serve, not just about them, but really to know them.

In our next section, we will get super practical with this concept of Servant-Minded Leadership!

# *Section 4*

## *Putting Servant-Minded Leadership into Practice*

There's an old saying: **"Don't TALK about it; BE about it!"** This sentiment resonates deeply with me. Too many leadership books focus on theory without offering practical guidance. My goal is to ensure that this book does not fall into that category.

In the first three sections, we explored the original value of Servant Leadership, how it was hijacked by a focus on organizational benefits, and how Servant-Minded Leadership offers a fresh opportunity to create a meaningful impact. Now, it's time to move from theory to action. In this section, we'll explore practical steps to bring these principles to life.

By the end of this section, my hope is that you'll feel empowered to put this book down but not the concepts within it. Instead, may you feel equipped, inspired, and ready to step forward as a Servant-Minded Leader.

So, let's get to it!

# Chapter 17

## Servant-Minded Leaders Have Mentors

*"The greatest gift is not being afraid to question."*
— *Marie Curie*

When I first set out to empower leaders vocationally, I began researching what resources could set me up for success. What I found was both alarming and discouraging. While dozens of programs promised to make me a wildly successful coach, the more I researched them, the more I realized that the people running these programs were not actually offering what was truly needed. I recall speaking to one individual who had spent over $16,000 to complete one of these programs. Sadly, they confirmed my suspicions. While they certainly learned things, it was nothing like what had been promised.

Before I continue with this chapter, I want to clarify two things:

1.   This is **NOT** a pitch for why you should hire me or my company.

2.   I am **NOT** recommending a coach.

This chapter is about *mentorship*. While our coaching is much more personalized than most, every leadership coach is limited in how much we can impact your life. What I am advocating for in this chapter is mentorship! Let me explain why mentorship can have so much greater of an impact.

Think back to your school days. Whether it was a coach or a teacher, the person investing in you also had many others who were demanding their attention. The teacher had an entire classroom, and the coach had an entire team. So, what were they good at? They were skilled at keeping everyone moving forward together. Whether it was a lesson plan for graduation or a game plan for a championship, they set clear goals and objectives and helped ensure that you achieved them. However, what they did not do, as a rule, was take a deep personal interest in you as an individual. Their schedules simply did not allow them to be more than superficially involved in your life.

If you're thinking, *"Hey! That's not true! I had a coach or teacher who invested specifically in me!"* then you are even more aware of how rare that is and how much of their personal time they had to sacrifice to do so. I would argue that if this happened for you, the individual actually stepped out of their teacher/coach role and into a mentorship role, especially during those after-class or after-practice moments when they were solely focused on you.

> *"Mentors are like the tutors and trainers of your school days. Coaches are like teachers and team coaches."*

So, who normally provides one-on-one attention? Typically, trainers and tutors. They knew what you struggled with in math and helped you avoid reinjuring your knee after last season's debacle. They stood with you throughout your journey. While they may not have been great at setting big-picture goals, they were incredibly helpful in the individual moments of your journey.

Mentors are like the tutors and trainers of your school days. Coaches are like teachers and team coaches.

There is tremendous value in coaching, and we offer a highly personalized version of it. But in this chapter, we are talking about something different. Servant-Minded Leaders need—and are mentors!

## The Power of a Mentor

After sifting through dozens of coaching programs, having many meetings, and realizing that half of them were fraudulent while the other half weren't what I needed, I became intentional about finding a mentor. The mentor I found was a man named Brent, and he was fantastic! Having been in leadership for over 40 years—including time as a college president, a member of the CEO Forum, and various other prestigious roles—Brent had both the experience and the passion for leadership. (He has also graciously written the forward for this book.)

I won't bore you with my personal journey, but I do want to share why having a mentor is a practical way to engage in Servant-Minded Leadership.

## Why Mentors Matter

### 1. Mentors Provide a Third-Party Perspective

No matter how much we want to be great leaders or how much we study books like this one, when we are deep in the trenches of leadership, we need an outside voice to keep us on track. Asking for guidance is not a sign of weakness or inadequacy it is an act of wisdom. A mentor provides valuable insights and ensures that the principles of Servant-Minded Leadership are being effectively implemented.

## 2. Mentors Have Already Walked the Path

Your mentor should not be a friend with the same level of experience as you. While a friend might be an outside voice and offer feedback, the best mentors have already accomplished what you are working toward. They have traveled the road ahead and can speak from experience, not just from hypothetical opinion.

## 3. Mentors Help You Work Through Your Thoughts

Have you ever planned to say something, only to have it come out completely wrong? If so, you understand the value of a mentor who listens and helps you process your thoughts. While anyone can be a sounding board, a mentor provides discernment, which is incredibly valuable when leading others.

### How to Find a Mentor

The value of a mentor is greater than words can express. But where can you find such a valuable resource? I have multiple mentors for different aspects of my life—a leadership mentor, a life/relationship mentor, etc. However, selecting them was not done through a Google search or some other equally misguided process. Instead, I asked myself three key questions:

1. **Who do I know that I respect?**
2. **Who do I know that has accomplished what I want to achieve?**
3. **Who do I know that would be willing to invest in my success?**

The order of these questions is crucial. If you mix up the order, you might end up with someone willing to help you, but not in the direction you actually want to go. Or you may respect someone, but they haven't walked the path you want to travel.

I don't know about you, but my list of people I genuinely respect is pretty small. I show respect to everyone, but the list of those I hold in high regard is short. If your list is long, asking *"Why do I respect this person?"* will likely narrow it significantly.

Once you have a list of people you respect, the next step is to ask, *"Who on this list has accomplished what I hope to achieve?"* If no one fits that description, you may need to expand your circle. Never sacrifice respect, but if no one in your life is ahead of you on your desired path, your growth is limited. It is always a good idea to surround ourselves with people who have already been where we want to go.

When you find someone who meets both criteria—someone you respect and who has walked the road you wish to travel—it's time to see if they are willing to mentor you. This can be intimidating. It may feel like dating all over again—asking someone to invest their time in you can be terrifying. But it is so worth it. And just like dating, you may hear several "no's before you get a "yes." However, when you do find that mentor, the effort will be well worth it.

Leadership coaches are everywhere. The more you pay, the more access you get. They play an important role in many lives. But Servant-Minded Leaders want something deeper—they seek mentors. Someone they respect. Someone who has accomplished their goals. Someone willing to share their wisdom and experience.

The role of a mentor cannot be overstated. They help sift through our thoughts, provide invaluable guidance, and offer an external perspective. Selecting the right mentor takes effort, but the rewards are immeasurable.

I recommend doing one of two things:

Pause reading until you have identified a mentor or,

Continue reading, but return to this chapter once you have found one.

For help in this area, please send an email to resources@servantmindedleadership.com and request a free copy of our Mentor Selection Worksheet. I'd love to ensure that you have this powerful resource as you seek the best mentor for your personal journey.

# Chapter 18

## Servant-Minded Leaders Get Started

*"The journey of a thousand miles begins with one step."*
— ***Lao Tzu***

Too many people avoid leadership roles because they feel they "aren't ready." The truth is, just as no one is ever truly "ready" to be a parent, we're never fully prepared to be a leader. But that doesn't exempt us from the responsibility. Whether you already hold an official leadership position and feel overwhelmed or need to step up due to a lack of effective leadership around you, the time to start is NOW.

There will always be more to learn, areas to improve, and challenges to overcome. In just a few chapters, I'll provide a list of things to focus on. But for now, stop making excuses and start implementing the principles of Servant-Minded Leadership.

The first step is simple: DECIDE to be a Servant-Minded Leader. The power of choice is incredible, and I encourage you to make that decision today. Commit to embodying these principles. You don't have to be perfect, just persistent. Keep trying, and you will succeed.

However, I must be honest with you. Choosing to be a Servant-Minded Leader is not a one-time decision. I wish it were that easy.

We could read a book, decide to be a great leader, and suddenly become one, but leadership requires ongoing commitment.

Every day, we must wake up and choose to lead effectively. And then, 20 minutes later, when our children don't listen, we must make that decision again. When a co-worker frustrates us or a neighbor test our patience, we must choose once more. The process continues at lunch, in meetings, during a break, on the way home, and in the evening. The decision to be a great leader is not a singular moment but a series of choices made throughout the day. True leadership is a continuous, intentional effort to positively impact the world. Since this is an ongoing commitment, it must be built on a solid foundation. And I believe that the foundation is love. When I say love is the foundation of Servant-Minded Leadership, people interpret it differently. So let me clarify.

**What I do NOT mean** is that leaders should love their people by saying yes to every request or doing everything people ask of them. Leadership isn't about pleasing everyone; it's about making the best decisions for the team, even when those decisions are difficult. Sometimes, love means saying "no" when something isn't aligned with the bigger picture or the health of the organization. The key is to check our motives and ensure that our decisions truly serve others rather than just serving our preferences.

> *"The decision to be a great leader is not a singular moment but a series of choices made throughout the day."*

**What I DO mean** is that great leaders have a general love for people. They see others as inherently valuable and worthy of respect. They recognize potential even in those who don't see it in themselves. They want the best for the people they lead.

This love should be most evident in our interactions with our team. If we believe that all humans deserve respect and value, then our team members who contribute to our mission daily should feel that appreciation in a dynamic way. They should know they are valued and their contributions matter.

Once we commit to leadership and cultivate a love for others, the next step is setting simple, actionable goals.

In the final section of this book, I'll outline four major goals for great leadership. For now, I want to emphasize the importance of decisive action. Vague intentions like "I will do better" won't lead to real improvement. Even with love as motivation, progress requires tangible steps.

A good goal should follow the *TNT Method*:

1. **Time-Oriented** – The goal must have a deadline. Instead of saying, "I'll do this eventually," set a timeframe like "one meeting per week" or "35 conversations by year-end." A time-based goal helps track progress and maintain accountability.

2. **Narrow(ed)** – The goal must be specific, targeted, and well-defined. Instead of saying, "I will make more money this year," a targeted goal would be: "I will have 35 one-on-one conversations with floor staff." A precise goal allows you to measure success.

3. **Temperate** – The goal should be challenging but realistic. It should stretch you without being overwhelming. For example, committing to personally connect with every employee in a 2,000-person organization may be unrealistic. However, setting a goal of one meaningful meeting per week is achievable and impactful.

By setting TNT goals, we will find that our decisions are infused with power, and we are able to achieve more than we thought possible.

Becoming a Servant-Minded Leader is a journey, but it's not an impossible one. The key is to focus on three fundamental steps:

1. **Commit to getting started.**
2. **Cultivate a genuine love for people.**
3. **Set simple, actionable T.N.T. goals.**

If we follow through on these steps, we will find ourselves stepping into our full potential as great servant-minded Leaders. In the next chapter, we'll explore strategies to ensure success in this journey.

# Chapter 19

## Doing What It Takes as a Servant-Minded Leader

*"The future depends on what you do today."*
— *Mahatma Gandhi*

There's an old story about three frogs sitting on a log. One decides to jump off.

How many frogs are left?

*Three.*

Why? Because deciding to do something isn't the same as actually doing it. It's only the first step. Important? Yes, but not the real thing.

That might seem simple, almost too obvious, yet it perfectly illustrates what separates those who lead from those who merely talk about leadership.

Years ago, I met a young woman who dreamed of becoming a nurse. By the time she turned twenty, she planned to be working in a hospital, caring for patients, and making a difference. She had the passion, the drive, and even a detailed plan.

But when she turned twenty, she hadn't even started nursing school.

Not because she lacked ability. Not because she changed her mind.

She simply didn't take the necessary steps. And that, more than anything, is what determines success or failure, not desire, not ambition, but action.

This truth applies just as much to leadership.

In the last chapter, we explored the foundational principles of Servant-Minded Leadership. But if all you do is read about them, if you don't act, then none of it will matter.

Commitments don't change lives. Actions do.

**Drawing the Line—Making a Real Commitment**

If you are ready to be a Servant-Minded Leader, I want to challenge you to do something right now. Not later, not tomorrow, but right this moment. I would like to invite you to join many others who have made this commitment to themselves and others. To do this, you will need the following:

> *"Servant-Minded Leaders are the ones who show up early, stay late, and do whatever needs to be done for the sake of their team."*

1. A dusty or sandy area.
2. A stick of some sort

If you're in a place where you can, grab a stick and find a patch of dirt or sand. If that's not an option, use your finger and a smooth surface with dust on it anything that allows you to physically draw a line.

Take the stick and mark a clear, visible line in the sand. On one side, write "Servant-Minded Leadership" (or just "SML" if space is tight).

Before you proceed, pause.

Look down at that line. Think about everything you've learned about leadership, about service, about the impact you want to have. Ask yourself: *Am I truly ready to commit?*

If the answer is yes, then take a deep breath, step over that line, and say out loud:

*"I commit to be a Servant-Minded Leader. I recognize I am uniquely positioned to impact those I lead, and I will work diligently to ensure that impact is positive. I will love my people, and I will serve them to the best of my ability."*

That step may seem small. But it isn't.

It's a defining moment. You've literally drawn a line in the sand and verbally declared who you are!

## Public Declarations and Accountability

A personal commitment is powerful. But a public one? Even more so. Once you've stepped over that line, tell someone about it. Let them know intend to change how you lead. Share how you are committed to being a Servant-Minded Leader. But, don't tell just anyone—tell the right people.

*Your team should know.* The people you serve should be aware that you are dedicating yourself to this path. Leadership isn't about secrecy; it's about accountability. If you're hesitant to share, ask yourself why.

*Your mentor or coach should know.* If you've followed the guidance in previous chapters, you've already sought out mentorship. Let them in on this decision. They will help you stay the course. And if you don't have a mentor yet, don't wait any longer. Find one!

*Your close friends and trusted peers should know.* Surround yourself with those who believe in Servant-Minded Leadership. If no one in your immediate circle fits that description, email me. I'd love to hear about your commitment and encourage you on this journey.

But, why does sharing your commitment matter?

Because words have power. And the moment you tell others, they will start holding you to it—sometimes in ways you don't expect.

One day, when you're frustrated, when you slip up, or when you're about to take the easy way out, someone will remind you.

"Didn't you say you wanted to lead differently?"

"I thought you were supposed to serve us, boss."

"Is that the kind of leader you want to be?"

It might sting in the moment, but that kind of accountability is exactly what will keep you on track.

**Action Over Perfection**

Too often, we wait for the perfect moment to start. We think we need more time, more training, more clarity. But the truth is, you don't need permission to lead.

- You don't need a title.

- You don't need a board meeting.
- You don't need a fresh calendar year.
- You just need to start.

Servant-Minded Leadership isn't about perfection. It's about showing up, consistently, with a heart for your people. It's about making the decision, over and over again, to put others first.

You've drawn the line. You've stepped over it. You've made your commitment known.

Now it's time to do the work.

Your team is waiting. Your influence is needed.

And the time to lead is today.

# Section 4

## *Conclusion*

The Servant-Minded Leader doesn't settle for theory. Reading about leadership isn't enough; we crave action, real transformation, and the ability to make a lasting impact on those we serve. We don't just acknowledge the responsibility of leadership; we embrace it fully, eager to step forward and put our principles into practice.

It begins with a declaration, spoken aloud. Whether in a quiet moment of personal reflection or in front of a group, this commitment marks the turning point between intention and action. And by making it known, we invite accountability, not as a burden, but as a tool for growth. Those around us will see our resolve, and in return, they will hold us to the standard we have chosen. True leadership is not practiced in isolation.

This is why we surround ourselves with those who will challenge and support us, mentors, colleagues, and friends who share our vision and won't hesitate to remind us of it when we falter. Leadership, after all, is a lifelong journey, and even the strongest leaders need encouragement. Having people who will speak truth to us, especially in difficult moments, keeps us aligned with our purpose.

Most importantly, we don't wait for the perfect moment to begin. There will always be reasons to hesitate, to postpone, to make excuses, but waiting serves no one. We take ownership of our leadership now. We step forward today. And as we do, we transform not only ourselves but those we serve, shaping a culture of trust, accountability, and action. This is what it means to be a Servant-Minded Leader.

# *Section 5*

## *A New Form of Leadership: Steps for Immediate Action*

Nothing stands in the way of success quite like uncertainty. Not knowing what to do can halt even the strongest desire to achieve something great. Imagine, for example, that I want to build a classic car. I've told people about my plans, maybe even set a few simple goals: "Find the right parts," "Develop a schedule." But there's one big problem: I don't actually know how to build a car. Sure, I can change a tire or swap out my oil if I have to, but when it comes to assembling a car from the ground up, I'm lost. If I truly want to succeed, I need guidance. I need someone who has done this before, someone who knows the process and can teach me where to start.

Leadership is no different.

Many leaders find themselves in positions they didn't necessarily ask for, and for which they weren't fully prepared. They have the passion, the drive, and the willingness to learn, but much like me, standing in front of a pile of car parts, they have no idea where to begin. They want to lead well, but they're floundering, trying to figure out what it actually looks like.

This section is for them. It's both for the seasoned leader looking to refine their abilities and the brand-new leader who is wondering, *What in the world do I do next?* Whether you've been leading for years or stepping into a leadership role for the first time, this section will walk through four key strategies that can be put into practice immediately—four foundational steps that will help you construct your own "car" of Servant-Minded Leadership.

But there's more. Beyond the strategies, we'll explore a critical next step, one that often determines whether leadership remains a short-lived experiment or becomes a lasting, meaningful legacy. My hope is that these insights will not only equip us with practical tools but also inspire us to embrace leadership as the life-changing opportunity that it is.

As you engage with this section, I invite you to do so with focus and intentionality. It can be tempting to rush through, eager to reach the end of the book, but may I suggest a different approach? Rather than powering through, consider reading one chapter per day or even one per week so each strategy has time to settle in and take root. Leadership isn't about information; it's about transformation. And transformation takes time.

This book is sub-titled *How Mindfulness Changes Servant Leadership* for a reason. Mindfulness requires presence, patience, and practice. We cannot fully absorb the principles of leadership if we are racing to finish the pages.

So, are you ready? Then, at your own best pace, let's begin.

# Chapter 20

## *I Love You*

*"People don't care how much you know until they know how much you care."*

— ***Theodore Roosevelt***

When I first introduced this concept, I mentioned how it had stirred controversy among some leadership experts. What I didn't mention is that, despite being debated, loving our people is not just a leadership preference; it is a necessity. It is the foundation of effective leadership, the core principle that should guide us every single day. This is not an occasional trait or a leadership style that we turn on and off. It is a continuous reality that must be evident in every exchange, in every decision, and in every action.

We have already discussed the topic of loving our people. But what does it actually mean to love our people? This is a crucial question because without understanding its practical application, we remain stuck in theoretical discussions. Talking about Servant-Minded Leadership is easy, but actually living it out is what defines true leadership.

There are two guiding principles that define love in leadership:

1. **Do unto your team as they would like you to do unto them.**
2. **Do unto your team what is best for them.**

111

Before moving on, take a moment to re-read these two statements.

Did you read the first one incorrectly at first glance? Did you assume it said, "Do unto others as you would have them do unto you"? If so, you're not alone. Many people instinctively default to the Golden Rule, a principle that has been ingrained in us since childhood. But I have intentionally altered it here, and for good reason. If you need to, please take a moment to go back and reread it, so that you know what I actually said.

**Understanding What People Need, Not What We Want**

For years, the Golden Rule has been applied to leadership: "Treat others the way you want to be treated." It is a great general principle, particularly in situations where we lack personal knowledge of someone. In ambiguous social settings, it can serve as a useful guideline. However, in leadership, it falls short.

Why? Because effective leadership requires *intentional understanding*. Our relationship with our team should not be casual or surface-level. We should be actively getting to know them, their values, their preferences, their struggles, and their aspirations.

> *"Effective leadership requires intentional understanding."*

Let me illustrate this with a simple analogy.

I love milk chocolate; the milkier, the better. My wife, on the other hand, is a dark chocolate enthusiast. If I were to follow the traditional Golden Rule and get her a treat, I might buy her milk chocolate, because that's what I would enjoy. However, as her husband, I should know better. I should recognize her preference and get her dark chocolate instead.

The same applies to leadership. When we first step into a leadership role, gestures like bringing in donuts for the team may seem like a nice touch. But if, after a month, we continue bringing donuts without realizing that one team member is gluten intolerant, another is on a strict diet, and a third simply doesn't like sweets, then we've missed the mark. What we *think* is a kind gesture becomes inconsiderate when we fail to acknowledge the unique needs of those we serve.

Consider a real example from my experience. I once organized an event for a group of college students, hoping to offer them something beyond their typical ramen noodles and energy drinks. We had a variety of foods, including sushi, sliders, and a shrimp ring. When one of the students arrived, she nearly had a heart attack—she was *highly* allergic to shellfish. Fortunately, she understood that I had no way of knowing that beforehand, and we quickly removed the shrimp.

But here's the key difference: If I had hosted another event with the same students and still included shrimp, knowing her allergy, my actions would have shifted from *an innocent mistake* to *an outright failure to care*. The lesson? Leadership requires us to move beyond generic gestures of kindness. It calls us to personalize our approach and truly understand what each person values.

**Love Requires Balance: Doing What's Best for the Team**

While it is important to treat people in a way that aligns with their preferences, leadership also requires another essential aspect of love: doing what is *best* for the team. This is the necessary balance in Servant-Minded Leadership.

At its core, love means doing what is best for another person, even at personal cost. While part of this involves meeting people where they are, it also requires making difficult decisions that may not be popular in the moment.

Let's be honest—people don't always *want* what is best for them. Sometimes, they resist growth, change, or discipline, even when it's in their best interest. As leaders, it is our responsibility to guide them forward, even when they don't see the value right away.

For instance, I once led a team that needed to significantly increase its workload. They were not happy about it. I was the new boss, and they saw me as the person making their easy job *much harder*. But I knew something they didn't—the company was restructuring, and they had less than a year to prove their value or risk being let go. My job was not just to make them comfortable; it was to prepare them for long-term success.

At first, they resisted. But over time, as they saw the results of their hard work and the security it brought them, they understood that my leadership wasn't about making their lives harder—it was about ensuring they had a future.

**Loving Leadership in Action**

Servant-Minded Leadership isn't just about bringing the right snacks or making people feel good in the moment. It is about being the leader your team *needs*, not necessarily the leader they *want* in any given situation.

Sometimes, leading with love means putting our egos aside and celebrating the achievements of others. Other times, it means aligning team members with tasks that suit their strengths and passions. And sometimes, it means making tough decisions that will benefit the team in the long run, even if they don't see it right away.

Ultimately, the foundation of loving leadership is *understanding that our team is not us*. They have different preferences, experiences, and goals. It is our job to invest in knowing them deeply, serving them intentionally, and making decisions that prioritize their well-being, even when it's not the easy or popular choice.

Love in leadership is a balance. We serve our team both in the way they *prefer* and in the way that is *best* for them. And when those two are in conflict, true leadership chooses what is best—because real love is not about keeping people comfortable; it is about helping them grow.

# *Chapter 21*

## *I'm Here for You*

*"The greatest gift of leadership is a boss who wants you to be successful."*

— *Jon Taffer*

Jason was a young leader who was always on the move. He was constantly doing something and was what most of us would consider a productive and proactive individual. He was so occupied with great things, in fact, when his mother would call with an invitation to dinner, he would rarely oblige the request.

*"So sorry, Mom," he would say. "I have so much going on this week! We'll make it happen soon!"*

This went on for months, with Jason not having a single night available to spend with his mother due to work and other business commitments. But then something curious happened.

Jason met Alexa.

After talking for a few minutes, he asked her out to dinner. They had a lovely time, and he asked her out the next night… and the next… and the next.

What happened?

Jason's business obligations were no different. In fact, they may have been even *more* pressing. What changed was Jason's priorities. Despite previously having no time for dinner with family, when Jason met Alexa, dinner became an open option and not just for one day, but for several days in a row!

Through Jason's life, we can learn a very important leadership lesson: **We HAVE time for what we MAKE time for.** This can be further explained by saying: **We HAVE time for what we WANT to make time for.** And almost always, the way we invest our time reflects the priorities in our lives.

> *"We have time for what we make time for."*

I love Laura Vanderkam's saying:

*Instead of saying, "I don't have time," try saying, "You're not a priority," and see how that feels.*

This is a hard truth for many of us. In fact, you may be thinking to yourself, *"Jon, that's not true. I love my spouse and want to spend more time with them. I just don't have the time!"*

If this is you, I don't question whether you love your spouse. However, I *do* believe that if you don't have time for them, you love something else *more*. Maybe it's work. Maybe it's volunteering. Maybe it's friends, social status, money, or something else. But whatever it is, we will make time for the things that are most important to us.

## What Does This Have to Do with Leadership?

This is not a marriage book, nor am I trying to force anyone to spend more time with their mom (although I'm sure she'd *love* it if you called once in a while).

So, what's all this about time management and priorities?

It has been said *"Time is the currency of love."* Yet too many leaders use the excuse of *"I just don't have time."* as the reason for their poor leadership practices.

What I hope you will take from this chapter is that, if we truly love our team, we will make time for them. We will be available.

Being available seems easy. In fact, most leaders will say that they are "available." And, while I am sure some still do, for the most part, I am thankful the days of leaders walking into work, shutting their office doors, and expecting their subordinates not to disturb them are largely gone.

And yet, while "open-door policies" are more common, most leaders are not *truly* available to their team. They may *think* they are, but in reality, that is often not the case.

I could spend a great deal of time on this subject if we were to diverge into the topic of **approachability,** which is a major component of availability. But I'll try to stick to the topic at hand. However, I *do* recommend checking out the video series on approachability on the *Servant-Minded Leadership* YouTube channel.

For now, let me just share another story that illustrates a leader with the best intentions, who still was not available.

## The Story of Cindy

I recall a director (we'll call her Cindy) who genuinely believed in the value of being available and accessible to her team and truly wanted to ensure they could always come to her.

But they didn't.

It was all too common that she was not approached until a problem had gotten so out of hand that she was forced to do damage control. This was terribly frustrating for her, as she regularly reminded her staff she was available and *wanted* to help!

One day, as Cindy was conducting an exit interview, the woman before her shared the reasons she was choosing to leave. Overcome with frustration, Cindy blurted out:

**"Why?! Why didn't you come to me? Why didn't you let me work on this? THIS ALL COULD HAVE BEEN SOLVED!"**

The young woman lowered her head and softly said:

*"I tried. I mean... I wanted to. I really did. But every time I came over to your office to talk to you, the door was closed, or you were on a call, or you seemed really busy, and I didn't want to bother you."*

After the former employee left her office, Cindy took some time to reflect on where things went wrong. Instead of dismissing the complaints, Cindy was wise enough to recognize they were *symptoms* of a deeper issue.

She realized that she had a tendency to schedule most of her meetings in the morning so she could have the rest of the day to focus on other tasks. Because of this, when she arrived, she would go straight into her office and close the door to avoid disrupting others during her meetings. While this wasn't *wrong*, the problem was that things would often press for her attention, and the day would pass by without her ever opening her door.

While her words said she was available, her actions shouted:

***"CAN'T YOU SEE I'M BUSY?! LEAVE ME ALONE!"***

It was never her intention to be unavailable, yet that was exactly what happened. And because of that, her entire organization suffered.

The first practical move of a **Servant-Minded Leader** (to love your team) will motivate and assist with the subsequent disciplines, including this one!

When we want what is best for our team and are willing to meet them on their terms, we will be empowered to make ourselves available to them. However, this requires a high level of intentionality and discipline.

Availability does not happen accidentally. In fact, it only happens through intentional effort!

So, how can we ensure we are *truly* available to our team? Here are three suggestions:

**1. Have Dedicated and Disciplined "Open Door" Hours**

I've found the best way to ensure availability is to schedule it. When I was directing several departments, my staff knew that from 1-3 PM every Friday, I was "twiddling my thumbs" during open-door hours—unless they came to talk to me. If they didn't, I would go to them.

## 2. Make the Space Inviting and Open

Your environment should make people feel *welcomed and valued.* Maybe this means a candy bowl, a putt-golf game, or simply ensuring the space is well-lit and uncluttered. Most importantly, it means giving undivided attention when someone enters the room.

## 3. Celebrate Those Who Take You Up on Your Offer

When the first brave soul hesitantly walks into your office celebrate it! Whether it's a simple "thank you," immediate action, or public acknowledgment, they should *feel* like they did the right thing by coming to you.

There are many ways to show availability, but the one constant is that our team *knows* we are there for them, that their time is just as valuable as ours, and that they are a priority.

Availability is not easy, but since when has leadership ever been easy?

# Chapter 22

## Are You Even Listening?

*"To be a leader, you must be a servant first."*
— ***Robert K. Greenleaf***

Has it ever happened to you? You're in the middle of a conversation, but your mind has drifted. As the final words of their sentence come out of their mouth, you are jarred back to the present. You instantly feel anxious as sweat starts to form on your brow. As you fumble to respond, you know exactly what the next humiliating question will be:

**"Are you even listening to me?"**

Why does that question strike such terror in our hearts? Well, frankly, because most of the time, we were *not* listening in the moments leading up to the inquiry. And we are well aware that to say *no* is to communicate that the person in front of us is not important enough to pay attention to. On the other hand, to say *yes* is to invite the next inevitable question:

**"Then what was I saying?"**

You are not alone. It's happened to all of us. Regardless of our intentions or the relevance of the person in front of us, we have all been in this position. But while this is something that happens to pretty much everyone, it doesn't make it acceptable for anyone, let alone a *Servant-Minded Leader.* Why? Because the third practical step of Servant-Minded Leadership is LISTEN.

This is not going to be a long chapter. There's really not much I need to say. It's quite simple:

**Leaders LISTEN.**

I don't mean leaders stand there while someone else talks. I don't mean leaders allow the sound of words to enter their auditory canal unobstructed. I mean a Servant-Minded Leader listens with the intent to understand and maybe even to learn.

If we love our team and make ourselves available to them, then the next logical step is that we will also listen to (and care about) what they have to say. We will *desire* to hear them not just their words, but also their hearts. We will *desire* to understand them. We won't assume we know more than they do. In fact, we will be disciplined enough to remember they have something to teach us.

> *"We will desire to hear them not just their words, but also their hearts."*

In my opinion, the number one reason we do not actually listen is that we think we already know everything we need to know. Of course, we would never say that. The idea that any of us would stop someone mid-sentence and say, "I already know everything I need to know, so you can stop talking," is laughable. And yet, think about it, if we truly believed they had something valuable to say, wouldn't we listen?

Think of the last time you were in a new place. You knew nothing and no one. You probably gave complete attention to your guide. Or maybe it was when you were in a new restaurant, and you listened intently to the waitstaff so you would know what to order. Whenever it was, there has probably been a time recently when you gave your full attention to someone. It may not have been your spouse or children, but it was *someone.* And the reason you listened so intently was that they had something to say that you did not already know or that you found valuable.

But when we are convinced, someone has something to tell us that we already know, we don't listen. We think about other things, we multitask, we tune them out. And then, when that dreaded question comes.

**"Are you listening?"**

**We panic.**

Do you know who doesn't need to panic when such a question is asked? The Servant-Minded Leader.

Why? Because they are happy to serve their team. They *actually* care about what the person is saying. They *want* to hear—not just their words, but also their hearts. Servant-Minded Leaders also know they don't know what they don't know. They are pleased to be present and take an authentic interest in the words and thoughts of the person with whom they are engaged.

This is the mark of a Servant-Minded Leader.

As I said, this is not a long chapter. But that's intentional. Since it is so short, can I make a recommendation? How about re-reading it? It won't take too long, but maybe the principles, even if they aren't new to you, will have a more dynamic impact if they are reviewed.

Whether you choose to re-read the chapter or not, let me leave you with this:

Servant-Minded Leaders **love** their people. With a heart of love, they make themselves available. And in the space of availability, they listen with a heart to understand.

# Chapter 23

## *Si, Ja, Oui, Sim, Evet, Tak, Da, 是的, はい, Yes*

*"The best way to predict the future is to create it."*
— ***Peter Drucker***

Quanelle was the kind of person every employee dreads encountering. For every solution, he had a problem. For every good idea, he had a reason why it wouldn't work. And even when he finally accepted changes, he was often the last to do so. He was, by all accounts, a nay-sayer, a no-finder, a Darryl-downer, and a roadblock to progress.

But here's the thing: Quanelle wasn't trying to be difficult. He genuinely believed he was helping. He wanted to ensure that resources weren't wasted on projects doomed to fail. He wanted to prevent his team from spending time on ideas he had already tried and dismissed. He aimed to bring clarity and focus to his team. And because he was analytical by nature, he had an uncanny ability to immediately pinpoint flaws in any proposal, believing he was saving time by eliminating impractical ideas upfront.

What he didn't realize was that in his pursuit of efficiency and productivity, he was slowly draining the enthusiasm, creativity, and initiative from his team. Without intending to, he made people feel small, disrespected, and unimportant.

So, what's the solution? Should Quanelle stop caring about efficiency? Should he hold back his expertise and experience? Is it really his problem if his team members can't handle having their ideas challenged? Many leaders wrestle with these very questions, believing that their role is to identify weaknesses and steer the team away from failure.

But this mindset—the "us vs. them" approach misses a crucial truth about leadership. Success in leadership is not about being "right" all the time. It's not about having all the answers or making sure others do things exactly as you would. In fact, the more quickly we accept that our way is not the only way or even the best way, the more effective we become.

You may recall from Chapter 15 a leader I once worked with who completely changed my thinking on this. They helped me see that allowing someone to complete a task in their own way often led to better results than forcing them to follow "my way." This wasn't just about allowing flexibility, it was about recognizing that different approaches could be just as, if not more, effective.

But the lesson doesn't stop there. Up until now, we've looked at this concept from the standpoint of a leader graciously "allowing" their team to operate with some autonomy. However, true Servant-Minded Leadership requires an even deeper shift: the realization that we might not even be right in the first place.

> *"Success in leadership is not about being 'right' all the time."*

Now, I can already hear the protests: *"Jon, come on! I know I'm not always right, but you can't expect me to assume I'm always wrong. I have years of experience! I've learned what works and what doesn't!"*

And you're absolutely correct. No one is saying that experience isn't valuable. The lessons we've learned over time are invaluable, and we should absolutely use them to guide and support our teams. But too often, that same experience turns us into another version of Quanelle. We believe we're helping when we immediately point out why something won't work, but in reality, we're crushing creativity and discouraging innovation. Over time, our team members stop bringing ideas forward—not because they don't have them, but because they don't see the point in trying.

That's why, as Servant-Minded Leaders, we must adopt a new mindset: *Find the Yes.*

We don't know what we don't know. The circumstances surrounding an idea may have changed since we last evaluated it. Technology may have evolved. Our team members may have skills and insights we lack. When we default to "no" because of our past experiences, we may be shutting down an opportunity for growth, innovation, or even success.

So yes, we should use our wisdom. Yes, we should guide our teams with the knowledge we've gained. But more than anything, we should be willing to listen—truly listen to understand and learn—before we dismiss an idea. Because sometimes, the best thing a leader can do is step back, embrace curiosity, and *find the Yes.*

Finding the "yes" is about shifting our mindset from rejecting ideas to exploring possibilities. It requires us, as leaders, to move beyond instinctive objections and instead cultivate an approach that prioritizes solutions over dismissals. This may feel unnatural, especially for those of us who have built our leadership styles on caution, efficiency, and risk management. However, embracing this mindset is one of the most powerful ways we can serve our teams, demonstrating that we respect their contributions and trust their ability to innovate.

Of course, saying "yes" does not mean abandoning discernment. There will always be moments when we must say "no"—due to budget constraints, company policies, or logistical barriers. However, these necessary "no's" should be the exception, not the rule. When we proactively seek to say "yes" as often as possible, our rare "no's" carry more weight and credibility.

So, how do we do this in practice? How do we "find the yes" in a way that is both genuine and sustainable? The answer lies in an essential leadership principle discussed in Chapter 16: Proper Nouns. Before we can truly embrace this approach, we must first understand the individuals we lead—their motivations, frustrations, and aspirations. Only then can we effectively serve them by finding solutions that align with both their needs and the organization's goals.

**The Power of Perspective**

One of the simplest but most effective ways to find the yes is to step into the shoes of the person making the request. When a team member presents an idea, rather than immediately evaluating its flaws, ask yourself:

*"If I were in their position, how would I go about making this work?"*

This shift in perspective can be incredibly revealing. In some cases, the idea may indeed be impractical. However, instead of shutting it down, we can engage in a conversation that allows for refinement and adaptation. One of the most empowering questions a leader can ask in these situations is:

*"That seems like a great idea. How do you think we should go about it?"*

This approach does (at least) two things:

1. **Encourages Ownership.** It challenges the individual to think critically about their proposal and actively contribute to its execution.

2. **Creates Collaboration.** Instead of positioning the leader as the ultimate decision-maker, it invites shared problem-solving, leading to stronger, more innovative solutions.

**Three Ways to Find the Yes**

While every situation is unique, there are three primary ways to ensure we are maximizing our opportunities to say yes:

**1. Simply Say Yes—and Follow Through**

Sometimes, the best approach is the simplest: just say yes. Far too often, leaders hesitate out of habit rather than necessity. If an idea is feasible and aligns with company objectives, don't overcomplicate it commit to it and see it through.

However, a critical component of this method is follow-through. A half-hearted yes that is later neglected or forgotten is worse than a straightforward no. Leaders should take intentional steps to ensure their commitments are honored. This could mean:

- Setting reminders in a calendar
- Assigning follow-up meetings
- Encouraging the person making the request to update leadership on progress

By doing so, we reinforce that our word carries weight and we genuinely support the initiatives brought forward by our team.

## 2. Adapt the Idea to Make It Work

Not every request can be accommodated exactly as presented but that doesn't mean the core idea must be rejected. Often, what people truly seek is not a specific outcome, but the fulfillment of an underlying need.

Consider a real-world example:

At one company, employees frequently requested permission to eat at their desks due to a small and overcrowded lunchroom. Management repeatedly declined the request, citing concerns about cleanliness and work-life balance. However, instead of focusing solely on the request itself, leadership took a step back and examined the need behind the request. The real issue was not a desire to eat at desks it was a lack of adequate space for breaks.

The solution? Instead of allowing desk lunches, the company invested in a larger, more comfortable break area. This met the employees' actual needs while maintaining the organization's workplace policies.

This example highlights an important lesson: Listen beyond the surface. Rather than focusing solely on the exact words of a request, take the time to understand the true challenge your team is facing and then work to find a solution to meets the need.

## 3. Empower Others to Create Their Own Yes

Perhaps the most impactful way to find the yes is to equip individuals with the tools and authority to make their own ideas a reality.

Rather than taking full responsibility for implementing a new initiative, leaders can turn the opportunity back to the person who proposed it by asking: *What steps can you take to bring this idea to life?"*

By doing so, we:

- **Foster innovation** by encouraging independent problem-solving.
- **Boost engagement** by allowing team members to take owner-ship of their ideas.
- **Build confidence** by showing trust in their abilities.

This not only strengthens the individual but also lightens the leader's workload, allowing the organization to grow dynamically rather than relying solely on top-down directives.

**Bringing It All Together**

Finding the yes is not just a leadership strategy, it's a mindset. It requires us to approach leadership from a place of service rather than control. And, as we've explored in previous chapters, this philosophy builds on the foundational principles of love, time, and listening.

When we love our people, we make time for them. When we make time for them, we listen to them. When we listen to them, they share ideas. And when they share ideas, we seek to find the yes.

This is how Servant-Minded Leadership transforms a workplace. It is how we inspire creativity, fuel engagement, and build a culture of trust and empowerment.

So, as you lead your team, challenge yourself with this question:

*What can I do today to find the yes?*

# Chapter 24

## OK, So What's Next?

*"The greatest gift is not being afraid to question."*
— *Marie Curie*

When I was growing up, my mother had a small pin on display. It was a gag gift she received when she graduated from college. The pin featured a character in graduation attire with the caption, "*Now that I know everything, what am I supposed to do?*" It was a humorous reminder that learning and growth never stop. Just because we finish a book, complete a certification, or even graduate, our development should never end.

This chapter explores the next steps for a Servant-Minded Leader. After putting these principles into practice, where do we go from here? How do we continue growing and leading effectively?

First, let me say that applying the principles in this book is already a huge step forward. One of the biggest mistakes people make when reading books like this is what I call "ascent without activation." We tend to mentally agree with the concepts, nodding along as if we understand, but then fail to apply them in real life. If you're actively using this book to become a more effective leader, I commend you for taking action and making a real impact on your team.

That said, this book isn't exhaustive. Eventually, you'll reach a point where you've absorbed what you can from its pages and wonder what's next. Of course, reading more books or taking additional courses are great next steps, and I encourage that. But before you move on, I have a suggestion.

Before seeking new knowledge, make sure you're applying what you already know as well as you think you are.

We would laugh at someone who believes they know everything just because they graduated. If someone truly thought that, we'd probably quiz them on the spot. Why? Because anyone convinced they have nothing left to learn likely lacks the perspective to recognize their own gaps. The same principle applies to leadership. Before assuming you've mastered these concepts, take the time to get some outside perspective on how well you're actually implementing them.

> *"No matter how good you think you are as a leader, my goodness, the people around you will have all kinds of ideas for how you can get better."*

That brings us to a crucial next step: feedback.

Feedback is an essential part of leadership. It offers insights we might otherwise miss and helps us refine our approach. Jim Yong Kim, former president of Dartmouth College and the World Bank, once said:

> *"No matter how good you think you are as a leader, my goodness, the people around you will have all kinds of ideas for how you can get better. So, for me, the most fundamental thing about leadership is to have the humility to continue to get feedback and to try to get better – because your job is to try to help everybody else get better."*

136

If someone who led one of the world's largest financial institutions valued feedback this much, then it's probably safe to say it's an essential part of leadership especially Servant-Minded Leadership. Leaders who dismiss feedback may hold positions of authority, but they lack the heart of a true leader.

Unfortunately, getting honest feedback isn't as easy as it should be. If you've embraced the principles of this book, then you likely understand the importance of feedback and might even be eager to ask for it. But enthusiasm alone isn't enough. I once knew a manager who, upon realizing that his team had unspoken concerns about him, showed up the next day and asked every employee if they had any issues with his leadership. While well-intentioned, his approach lacked wisdom. As we briefly discussed in Chapter 21, approaching a leader even with a simple question can be intimidating. Providing candid feedback is even harder.

I've personally worked with leaders I deeply respected, people who embodied Servant-Minded Leadership. And yet, when given the opportunity to provide feedback, I often hesitated. Not because of anything they did wrong, but because of my own insecurities. The reality is that positional authority can create an invisible barrier, making honest feedback difficult to obtain.

So, if feedback is so essential and yet so challenging to obtain, what can we do? Giving up isn't an option—it's simply too valuable. Assuming we're the exception is also dangerous. The best approach is to create an environment where honest feedback is encouraged and protected.

A simple three-step process can help:
1. Make it anonymous at first.
2. Celebrate participation.
3. Take action immediately.

**Make it anonymous at first.**

The first step in building a feedback culture is ensuring people feel safe sharing their thoughts. If team members fear repercussions, they won't be honest. An anonymous feedback system one where responses cannot be traced back to individuals is essential at the beginning. If our goal is genuine growth, then the source of the feedback shouldn't matter. What matters is that we receive it.

At SML Consultive, we've worked with organizations that prioritized authentic feedback. In these cases, we acted as an independent third party, collecting feedback and removing any identifying data before presenting the insights to leadership. This allowed leaders to get unfiltered, honest input without employees fearing backlash. Whether it's an anonymous suggestion box, a general email that anyone can send messages from, or a third-party survey, the key is ensuring the process is trustworthy and maintains the integrity of anonymity.

You may have noticed I said to make it anonymous at first. That doesn't mean pulling a bait-and-switch later. However, over time, as you prove feedback is valued and acted upon, people will become more comfortable offering direct input. But before that can happen, we need to address the next two steps.

**Celebrate participation.**

Celebrating participation is crucial in establishing a strong feedback culture. Since feedback is initially anonymous, you might wonder how to celebrate those who contribute without knowing who they are. The key is to celebrate the feedback itself. A simple, enthusiastic announcement about the first round of feedback being received and the excitement of learning and growing from it can have a meaningful impact. This effect is even stronger if you highlight specific feedback that was particularly insightful, demonstrating you are actively listening and valuing what is being shared.

This phase serves two important purposes. First, it reassures the team that this is not just another hollow feedback initiative. Many workplaces have "suggestion boxes" that are checked only occasionally, filled with old complaints, and rarely lead to real change. To build trust, your team must see that this process is different—that feedback is not only welcomed but acted upon.

Second, celebrating feedback helps spark conversation. If someone submits a comment about your hairstyle being distracting to clients, for example, how you handle it will determine whether the team truly engages in the process. If you openly acknowledge the feedback "We appreciate the suggestion about hairstyles and professionalism" it gets people talking. One might say, "Who said that? I've wanted to mention it for years! Maybe this feedback thing is real." This kind of discussion helps establish a workplace culture where people feel comfortable sharing honest opinions.

However, there is a common pitfall that leaders must avoid: the **DUDE** trap. This happens when we:

- **Defend** ourselves, our actions, or our decisions.
- **Undermine** the opinions given or the overall process.
- **Dismiss** a suggestion outright, either by disregarding the source or the recommendation itself.
- **Explain** our reasoning in a way that diminishes the feedback's value.

For example, if you receive feedback about your hairstyle and respond with, "I appreciate the feedback, but I've had this style since I was 16, and I'm not changing it now. Keep the feedback coming!" you've completely undermined the process. Even if you have a valid reason for keeping your hairstyle, your response sends the message that you are not actually open to change. The goal is to show that feedback matters, not just acknowledge it and then shut it down.

To build a true feedback culture, it's essential to welcome input without defensiveness. Celebrate participation, encourage ongoing dialogue, and make it clear that feedback isn't just collected, it leads to meaningful reflection and action.

**Take Action Immediately!**

The final step in building a strong feedback culture is also the most critical and the most often neglected. Feedback is meaningless if it doesn't result in real, visible change. In fact, ignoring feedback can make things worse by creating frustration and discouraging future participation. To prevent this, find something from the first round of feedback that you can act on right away. Even a small adjustment can serve as the foundation for a meaningful and effective feedback system.

When taking action, communication is key. Clearly share what change is being made and why. For example:

*"Good morning, everyone! I want to thank you all for the recent feedback. I see that my hairstyle may not be working well internally or externally. While I don't know who submitted this feedback, I want you to know that I'm listening. When I return on Monday, I will have visited my barber/stylist we'll see if a little change can make a big impact!"*

This type of response demonstrates that feedback is not just collected but actually leads to action, encouraging further participation and trust in the process.

## Not All Feedback is Feasible

While taking action is important, not all feedback can or should be implemented. Some suggestions may not align with the organization's mission or may be impractical. However, it's crucial to handle these situations carefully. If you start by rejecting ideas, trust is broken before the process even begins. Instead, first find something to say yes to, and only then address what can't be changed.

When declining a suggestion, always treat the feedback with dignity—even if it's harsh or unrealistic. Suppose someone submits feedback saying:

*"You are a terrible leader and should resign immediately."*

A natural reaction might be to dismiss or defend, but both responses would be counterproductive. Instead, respond in a way that acknowledges the concern while reinforcing your commitment to improvement:

*"Due to the truly anonymous nature of this feedback, I don't know who shared this. But I see that someone feels I am a terrible leader and should resign. First, I want to express my gratitude for your honesty. I take this very seriously. While I cannot step away from my responsibilities, I can and will work hard to be a better leader. If the person who submitted this would like to provide more specific feedback on areas where I can improve, I would genuinely welcome that."*

This approach achieves several things:

✓ It validates the feedback, showing that all input is valued.

✓ It identifies where change **is** possible while reinforcing necessary boundaries.

✓ It builds trust by demonstrating a commitment to growth rather than defensiveness.

**Not All Feedback is Valuable**

Some feedback will be rooted in frustration rather than constructive criticism. This is an unfortunate but inevitable aspect of an anonymous system. The best way to handle this type of feedback is by seeking clarification rather than reacting.

For example, if someone submits a complaint about office Christmas decorations, a productive response could be:

*"I want to thank the person who submitted their thoughts about our Christmas decorations. It seems like you have strong opinions on this, but I'm not entirely sure I understand the heart of your concern. I'd love to connect personally to better understand your perspective so we can explore appropriate responses."*

This response also accomplishes three things:

1. **It neutralizes the complaint**—most people who submit venting complaints do not want to be identified, so they are unlikely to follow up.

2. **It reinforces the culture of openness** by showing that even minor concerns are taken seriously.

3. **If the person actually follows up**, it signals that their concern may be more significant than it initially seemed, warranting further discussion.

**Evolving the Feedback Culture**

One final thought before diving into the 360° feedback model: anonymity should be a steppingstone—not the end goal. Initially, anonymity helps foster a safe space for honest feedback. But over time, as trust builds, the goal should be to transition toward a hybrid system where both anonymous and direct feedback are welcomed.

As this transition happens, all the principles discussed (celebration, action, trust-building) must remain in place. Feedback culture is not just about collecting opinions; it's about creating an environment where people feel heard, respected, and empowered to contribute to meaningful change.

Now, let's explore the 360° feedback model and how it can take this process to the next level.

**The 360° Feedback Model**

One of the biggest problems with most feedback mechanisms is that they are linear. Usually, feedback flows top-down, sometimes bottom-up, but neither approach creates the kind of feedback culture that truly benefits leaders or organizations. In a top-down system, feedback is given by superiors in structured, formal reviews, often once or twice a year. In a bottom-up approach, subordinates provide feedback more informally. While both have value, neither is complete on its own.

For feedback to be most effective, it must come from multiple directions, creating a well-rounded perspective that drives real growth. For leaders, the 360° feedback model includes four or five types of feedback, depending on whether external feedback is incorporated. These include self-reflection, subordinate feedback, supervisor feedback, peer feedback, and, when applicable, client feedback.

Self-reflection may seem unusual, but it is the foundation of the entire feedback process. If we are unwilling to be honest with ourselves, we are unlikely to accept authentic feedback from others. The first step is to assess ourselves critically, examining our strengths, weaknesses, and areas for improvement as if we were our own supervisor. Making excuses or ignoring problem areas renders the rest of the process ineffective. Many leaders avoid self-reflection, which makes them resistant to external feedback and stunts their growth.

Once self-feedback has been established, gathering subordinate feedback is the next step. While some leadership experts suggest leaders should seek feedback from their superiors first, subordinates often provide the most useful insights because they work with us daily and are directly impacted by our leadership. If we have cultivated a culture of open communication, their feedback will highlight patterns and behaviors that might otherwise go unnoticed.

Superior feedback follows. Unlike subordinate feedback, which tends to be detailed and situational, superior feedback is often broader and aligned with the organization's overall vision. While it may not focus on everyday interactions, it provides context for the leadership decisions we make. Balancing superior and subordinate feedback helps ensure that personal growth aligns with organizational goals.

Peer feedback is often overlooked, yet it is crucial in determining whether we are effective team players. A leader may be highly valued by their superiors for being a "company person," yet disliked by their team for being difficult to work with. Conversely, a leader might be well-loved by their team but misaligned with the organization's vision. More commonly, leaders maintain good relationships with both their superiors and their teams but struggle with peer relationships. This is especially true for Servant-Minded Leaders, whose commitment to excellence can sometimes create tension among colleagues. Peers may perceive ambitious, dedicated individuals as overly eager or insincere. However, their perspective is valuable in determining whether our actions and strategies benefit the organization as a whole.

An additional layer of feedback may come from clients. While leaders must focus on their internal teams, external clients are ultimately the reason businesses succeed or fail. If customers are not satisfied, they will not return, and eventually, there may be no team left to lead. Seeking client feedback, when possible, helps ensure that leadership decisions contribute to overall success.

Beyond these five feedback sources, mentorship plays a vital role in interpreting and applying feedback effectively. A mentor provides the necessary perspective to distinguish useful insights from less relevant ones, ensuring that feedback leads to meaningful improvement rather than confusion or frustration. While the 360° feedback model is powerful, it should never replace the guidance of an experienced mentor.

Lastly, none of this matters if feedback does not lead to action. Seeking input without making changes is a waste of time for everyone involved. While not every piece of feedback will be acted upon immediately, the overall mindset should be one of continuous growth and improvement. Leadership development requires effort, and authentic feedback is an essential part of that journey. It is not always easy to receive, but it is always worth it.

# *Section 5*

## *Conclusion*

The real value of any leadership book or any self-improvement resource is not in the words printed on the pages, but in what you choose to do with them. Too often, people consume knowledge without ever applying it, leading to the cycle my colleague described: new ideas that feel exciting in the moment but fade without meaningful change. I don't want that for you.

You've made an investment by reading this book, not just financially, but with your most valuable resource: your time. My hope is that this section has helped bridge the gap between theory and action, providing practical ways to implement these concepts into your daily leadership. Leadership growth isn't about one big breakthrough; it's about consistent, intentional steps forward.

I understand how easy it is to read a book, feel inspired, and then quickly move on to other responsibilities without taking the necessary steps to put ideas into action. Life gets busy. Other pressing matters demand your attention. Maybe you read this book over a weekend and, as soon as Monday rolls around, the realities of your job take over. Or perhaps this book has been a year-long journey for you, and some of the earlier concepts feel distant. That's exactly why I structured the next section the way I did to make it easy for you to revisit the key ideas and implement them in a way that fits your real-world leadership journey.

The following pages will provide a summary of each chapter. Each summary is designed to be a quick reference guide, allowing you to refresh your memory without rereading an entire chapter. I want this book to remain useful to you long after you've finished reading it. When you need to recall something specific, these summaries will help you find it quickly. And if you ever want to revisit a full chapter for more details, I've included page numbers to guide you directly to where each chapter begins.

This book was never intended to be something you simply read once and forget. It was designed to be a resource that you can return to time and time again, using it as a tool to refine your leadership skills and create a lasting impact. Theoretical knowledge is important, but without practical application, it holds little value. You now have the tools to implement what you've learned. The next step is yours to take.

So, as you continue through the next section, use it to reinforce your understanding and to ensure that the concepts in this book don't just remain ideas but become part of the way you lead. Keep pushing forward, keep refining your leadership, and most importantly, take action. That's how real growth happens.

# *Chapter Summaries*

# Summary of Chapter 1

### *The original idea of Servant Leadership* ~ (Page 3)

The original idea of Servant Leadership, though popularized by Robert K. Greenleaf's 1970 essay "The Servant as Leader," is a philosophy that existed long before, evidenced in the teachings of figures like Jesus, Aristotle, and ancient Buddhist traditions. At its core, Servant Leadership emphasizes the leader's primary role as a servant focused on the needs and well-being of their followers. This approach prioritizes the growth, development, and success of team members, contrasting sharply with traditional hierarchical models centered on authority and control. Key principles include empathy, active listening, building trust-based relationships, shared decision-making, empowerment, ethical behavior, and serving the greater good.

This leadership ideology rests on the foundation of human dignity and intrinsic value, aiming to positively impact the lives of others through empowering and loving influence. It actively pushes back against ego-centric or fear-based leadership styles that prioritize personal prestige over team success. Leaders who adopt this mindset seek to enable their followers to become their best selves, viewing themselves as facilitators working to create a supportive environment. This philosophical base is critical to understanding the pure intent behind Servant Leadership, setting the stage for discussions on its modern evolution and potential improvements.

**Key Takeaways:**

1. **Servant Leadership is rooted in historic wisdom.**

2. **It emphasizes humility, empathy, and empowerment.**

3. **Its impacts extend beyond individuals to benefit communities.**

# Summary of Chapter 2

*The Personal Impact of - SL (1970s and beyond)* ~ (Page 7)

Bringing Servant Leadership into a modern context involves exploring the influential voices who have shaped this philosophy over the last half-century. Leaders like John Maxwell, Dale Carnegie, and Simon Sinek have played a significant role in popularizing the principle that true leadership is fundamentally about empowering the team, not focusing on the leader themselves. This ethos has fueled the creation and dissemination of countless resources, including books, podcasts, and training programs, all centered around the idea of fostering leaders who act as advocates and champions for their teams.

Beyond these public figures, millions of unsung leaders embody Servant Leadership principles daily. These are individuals who prioritize the well-being of those they lead and influence through humility, encouragement, and direct personal impact. While their names may not be globally recognized, their actions create profound ripple effects within their immediate circles and communities. The enduring relevance and impact of Servant Leadership in the modern era are a testament to both the prominent advocates who amplify its message and the countless individuals who live out its principles in their daily interactions.

**Key Takeaways:**

1. **Modern advocates reinforce that true leadership serves the team, not the leader.**

2. **The philosophy thrives through both famous and unsung leaders.**

3. **Servant Leadership's impact endures through both influence and daily practice.**

# Summary of Chapter 3

*The Positive Impact of Servant Leadership ~ (Page 11)*

Since its popularization in the 1970s, Servant Leadership has had a broad and positive impact, fundamentally changing expectations and sparking a widespread conversation about what effective leadership entails. In stark contrast to previous eras where discussions around leadership principles were uncommon, the modern environment now expects leaders to actively consider employee well-being, empowerment, and open communication. This shift in dialogue is arguably the single most impactful contribution of Servant Leadership over the past six decades.

Even among leaders who may not fully embody its ideals, the concept of Servant Leadership has permeated organizational culture, creating a pressure to conform to its principles. This increased awareness and conversation have led to a greater expectation that leaders will lead well, fostering environments where people feel valued and heard. The ongoing discussion around Servant Leadership is seen as undeniably positive, motivating leaders to step up, develop others, and continue making a positive change in the world by improving the day-to-day working lives of employees.

**Key Takeaways:**

1. **Servant Leadership has reshaped leadership expectations.**

2. **The conversation now pressures leaders to consider team well-being.**

3. **The shift has created greater accountability and positive cultural change.**

# Summary of Chapter 4

*The Lasting Impact of Servant Leadership* ~ (Page 15)

Given its sixty-year history, a natural question arises about the future of Servant Leadership: is it merely a temporary trend, vulnerable to economic shifts, or does it possess enduring impact? While acknowledging that some leaders may quote Servant Leadership ideals without genuine commitment, the philosophy has undeniably influenced expectations and reshaped conversations surrounding leadership in the modern workplace. Servant Leadership, as a concept, has made a lasting splash, impacting what employees expect from those in charge.

Looking ahead, several factors suggest Servant Leadership is here to stay and likely to expand. There is a growing desire among both employees and leaders for authentically caring leadership. Furthermore, the commercial ecosystem surrounding Servant Leadership, including a multitude of books, seminars, and training programs, makes it deeply embedded in professional development. This significant momentum, coupled with the evident desire for leaders who genuinely prioritize their teams, points towards a future where the influence and implementation of Servant Leadership continue to grow, fostering more positive work cultures despite implementation challenges.

**Key Takeaways:**

1. **Servant Leadership has influenced leadership expectations and conversations.**

2. **Widespread support among leaders and employees suggests a lasting impact.**

3. **The philosophy's growth will likely foster more positive work cultures.**

# Summary of Chapter 5

*Servant Leadership is Not Bad ~ (Page 23)*

For readers anticipating a critique of Servant Leadership, this chapter clarifies that the intention is not to debunk the philosophy itself, but rather to build upon it. Servant Leadership, founded on the principle that leaders are called to serve their teams, is presented as a profoundly beneficial approach. It cultivates essential qualities such as empathy, shared growth among team members, and widespread empowerment throughout the organization. This focus on service fosters stronger collaboration, encourages ethical decision-making, and ultimately creates a more supportive and productive work environment.

The numerous benefits of Servant Leadership extend beyond team dynamics. Leaders who genuinely serve their teams facilitate enhanced employee engagement and loyalty, leading to increased productivity and reduced turnover, which in turn brings substantial ethical and financial returns for organizations and their clients. The empowerment fostered by Servant Leadership sets teams up for both short-term success and long-term development. Far from being problematic, the core idea of Servant Leadership is presented as a fantastic concept that promotes growth and positive impact at all levels.

**Key Takeaways:**

1. **Servant Leadership fosters empathy, growth, and empowerment.**

2. **Ethical leadership brings substantial returns for organizations and clients.**

3. **Empowered teams lead to higher satisfaction, retention, and productivity.**

# *Summary of Chapter 6*

Servant Leadership is Necessary ~ (Page 27)

Taking the argument a step further, this chapter asserts that Servant Leadership is not merely beneficial, but fundamentally necessary for the success of an organization from multiple perspectives. Regardless of one's position—from executives to front-line employees, and across functions like HR and Finance—the principles of Servant Leadership are crucial for achieving individual and collective goals and fostering overall happiness within the workplace.

For executives, Servant Leadership is necessary because it drives increased productivity and efficiency, which are paramount concerns. HR departments find it essential for improving employee retention and satisfaction, thereby reducing costly turnover and fostering a positive workplace culture. For employees, Servant Leadership combats the negative impacts of poor leadership, leading to greater well-being and engagement. Finally, for managers, it provides the tools and framework needed to effectively lead teams, support individual growth, and contribute to organizational success. Its necessity stems from its pervasive positive impact across all levels and aspects of an organization.

## Key Takeaways:

1. **Servant Leadership benefits all levels of an organization.**

2. **Leadership development improves retention and productivity.**

3. **Employees thrive under positive, empowered leadership.**

# Summary of Chapter 7

*So, What's Wrong with Servant Leadership?* ~ (Page 31)

Despite establishing Servant Leadership as both good and necessary, this chapter pivots to address its core issue: how its application has become skewed by an overemphasis on Return on Investment (ROI). While acknowledging that serving others inherently leads to positive outcomes like increased productivity and happier employees, the focus on these measurable results as the primary justification for Servant Leadership risks distorting its true value and pure intent. The widespread dissemination of Servant Leadership theories through paid channels like workshops, books, and speeches has inadvertently tied the philosophy's value proposition to its tangible benefits for the organization.

This shift means conversations around Servant Leadership often center on outcomes like increased revenue, decreased expenses, and improved retention, rather than the intrinsic value of serving people. When the primary narrative revolves around ROI, it becomes challenging to maintain the philosophy's original heart—a selfless commitment to the growth and well-being of others. This focus on measurable benefits, while understandable from a business perspective, is identified as the key factor that has led Servant Leadership to sometimes "miss the mark" of its intended purpose, necessitating a re-evaluation of its motive.

**Key Takeaways:**

1. **ROI can distort the true value of Servant Leadership.**
2. **Leadership development requires long-term cultural investment.**
3. **Serving others should be the focus, not just productivity metrics.**

# Summary of Chapter 8

*People, Progress & Profit* ~ (Page 37)

The common corporate adage, "Our staff are our greatest asset," is intended to highlight the importance of employees, but this phrase often implicitly links employee value directly to their contribution to the business's bottom line. The underlying idea is that employees who feel valued and appreciated will be more motivated, leading to increased productivity and, subsequently, greater profits. In this framework, employees can sometimes be viewed as assets that primarily contribute to the company's financial success, similar to other resources.

While companies may use words like "valued" and "appreciated," there is often a disconnect between this rhetoric and the actual actions taken to make employees feel genuinely cared for. This gap between stated values and practical implementation has fueled the development and adoption of various programs and strategies, including aspects of Servant Leadership, aimed at improving the employee experience and fostering greater engagement. The evolution of these leadership approaches reflects a need to better align organizational language about valuing people with tangible investments and actions that demonstrate true care beyond mere productivity metrics.

**Key Takeaways:**

1. **Employee appreciation is vital for productivity and morale.**

2. **Words of appreciation must be backed by actions to be effective.**

3. **Servant Leadership aims to better align employee recognition with true care.**

# Summary of Chapter 9

*Servant Leadership 2.0 ~ (Page 39)*

The evolution of workplace perks, famously pioneered by tech companies with amenities like unlimited snacks and recreational spaces, stemmed from the core idea of Servant Leadership: that leaders should serve their teams to remove obstacles and enhance their work environment. This early implementation aimed to boost employee satisfaction, creativity, and productivity by providing comforts and conveniences that went beyond traditional workplace norms. As this model spread, leadership development programs began to emphasize a broader application of service.

This expanded approach, dubbed "Servant Leadership 2.0" by some, called upon leaders not only to facilitate a comfortable environment but also to actively stand at the point of conflict, acting as advocates and protectors for their team. Leaders were encouraged to take extreme ownership of team results, reflecting credit onto their members while absorbing blame themselves. This focus on leader accountability and team protection, alongside the provision of workplace perks, became intertwined with the promise of increased productivity and engagement. This era saw Servant Leadership principles spark a massive industry centered on employee-focused solutions and leader development.

**Key Takeaways:**

1. **The concept of serving the team led to enhanced workplace amenities.**

2. **Modern programs encourage leaders to take ownership and create safe environments, empowering teams.**

3. **Servant Leadership principles have sparked a multi-trillion-dollar industry, with growing demand for employee-centered solutions.**

# Summary of Chapter 10

*Servant Leadership is Here to Stay* ~ (Page 43)

In a business landscape often characterized by the fleeting adoption of new initiatives, Servant Leadership has demonstrated remarkable longevity. Unlike many other programs that generate initial excitement but quickly fade, this philosophy has become deeply embedded in corporate culture over the past six decades. Its enduring presence is attributed not only to its positive impact on workplace dynamics and employee engagement but also, significantly, to its proven Return on Investment (ROI) in areas like improved retention and financial savings.

Few organizations today openly reject Servant Leadership; even those whose leaders struggle with consistent application often still promote the concept for its perceived benefits in team building and public image. The principles of Servant Leadership, particularly its connection to tangible business outcomes, are now so fundamental that companies rely on them as a framework for management and employee relations. While widely embraced for both its cultural and financial value, the ongoing implementation often remains tied to its measurable results. This sustained focus on ROI, while ensuring its continued presence, also highlights areas where the application of Servant Leadership may benefit from refinement.

**Key Takeaways:**

1. **Servant Leadership's endurance proves its cultural and financial value.**

2. **Organizations appreciate both the social and monetary ROI of Servant Leadership.**

3. **Despite its strengths, Servant Leadership may benefit from refinement.**

# *Summary of Chapter 11*

*What if the ROI is the Problem? ~* (Page 47 )

This chapter poses a critical question: Could the very emphasis on Return on Investment (ROI), which has contributed to Servant Leadership's widespread adoption, also be its central problem? Analogized to helping a friend move in exchange for payment, the core idea of Servant Leadership as a genuine act of service can be transformed into a mere business transaction when the focus shifts primarily to measurable returns. As organizations invest in leadership development, the prioritization of ROI often overshadows the authentic, selfless act of serving employees.

This outcome-driven messaging has permeated the conversation around Servant Leadership to such an extent that there is almost exclusive focus on the ROI, with little emphasis on the "servant" aspect. Leadership pitches and even AI definitions highlight collaboration, employee engagement, and organizational success as the main goals, implicitly linking service to these benefits. This perspective risks treating employees as assets primarily valued for their contribution to profit rather than individuals worthy of care for their intrinsic value. The chapter argues that while ROI is a necessary consideration for organizations, framing Servant Leadership predominantly around it has corrupted the noble ideal of service.

**Key Takeaways:**

1. **Overemphasis on ROI is undermining Servant Leadership's core purpose.**

2. **Authentic service requires focusing on employees as individuals, not assets.**

3. **Shifting from ROI-driven metrics to genuine care can revitalize the Servant Leadership model.**

# Summary of Chapter 12

*What is Leadership Mindfulness? ~* (Page 57)

Introducing the concept of "Servant-Minded Leadership," a mindful approach that shifts the focus back to authentic service rather than being driven primarily by ROI. Leadership mindfulness, derived from the definition of "mindful" as being conscious or aware of something, calls for a deliberate engagement with the core concepts of Servant Leadership, in contrast to the common awareness dominated by Return on Investment. This "minded" distinction encourages deeper questions about the true meaning and purpose of Servant Leadership.

Servant-Minded Leadership is explicitly defined as not being a rigid "program" or a "quick fix," acknowledging the ineffectiveness of one-size-fits-all solutions for unique individuals. Instead, it is presented as an ongoing commitment rooted in authentic love for others and a sincere desire to fulfill one's leadership responsibilities with excellence. It involves actively seeking what is best for team members, even if it's not what they initially want, and holding oneself to a high standard while empowering others with trust and necessary authority. This approach seeks to foster a culture built on genuine care and integrity, moving beyond transactional metrics to meaningful, people-centered engagement.

**Key Takeaways:**

1. **Servant-Minded Leadership emphasizes authentic love and care for individuals beyond programmatic solutions.**

2. **This approach prioritizes what's best for the team, not just what's convenient for the leader.**

3. **Servant-Minded Leaders pursue excellence, setting a high standard while empowering others with trust and support.**

# *Summary of Chapter 13*

*Question Everything* ~ (Page 65)

Crucial to Servant-Minded Leadership is the cultivation of curiosity, mirroring the persistent "why" questions asked by children. This innate drive for understanding often diminishes with age, but reviving the habit of asking questions is presented as essential for effective leadership. Questions such as "Why am I here?", "What is my purpose in this role?", and "How can I make a difference?" are vital for leaders to clarify their contribution, align their actions with their values, and gain a deeper understanding of their position and its potential impact.

Mindfulness in leadership extends beyond immediate tasks to understanding the broader implications of one's role and the potential impact on the lives of those being led and the organization as a whole. Asking these fundamental questions is an act of humility that opens the door to greater self-awareness and insight. This approach helps leaders move beyond assumptions and predefined roles, facilitating deeper engagement with their purpose. Continuously seeking understanding through questioning is foundational to Servant-Minded Leadership, strengthening the team and promoting intentional, impactful leadership.

**Key Takeaways:**

1. **Asking "why" leads to greater understanding and mindful leadership.**

2. **Leaders should clarify their purpose and impact within their role.**

3. **Servant-Minded Leaders continuously seek growth through curiosity.**

# Summary of Chapter 14

*I Don't Know What I Don't Know* ~ (Page 71)

Servant-Minded Leadership emphasizes mindfulness as the active awareness required to serve people authentically and fairly. This mindful approach means that serving others is not synonymous with agreeing to every request. Instead, it requires balancing empathy and the desire to help with careful judgment and a comprehensive understanding of the situation. Leaders may often assume that fulfilling every request will lead to team satisfaction, but this is rarely sustainable or truly beneficial in the long term. A mindful leader must always seek the full context, considering the needs of the broader team and the organization, not just individual perspectives.

Effective leaders approach each situation with the understanding that they "don't know what they don't know," recognizing their limited knowledge and actively seeking to learn more. This involves gathering insights from multiple sources and perspectives before making decisions, avoiding the pitfalls of acting solely on the first information received. Mindful leaders engage with team members genuinely, validating their humanity while thoughtfully evaluating the bigger picture. By continuously seeking input and acknowledging the inherent biases in individual accounts, Servant-Minded Leadership sustains meaningful, equitable service, fostering both trust and dignity within the team over time.

## Key Takeaways:

1. **Servant-Minded Leadership combines empathy with mindful decision-making.**

2. **Leaders should approach each situation with context and perspective.**

3. **Effective leaders acknowledge their limited knowledge and seek to learn more.**

# *Summary of Chapter 15*

*My Way or the Highway to the Byway* ~ (Page 75)

Servant-Minded Leadership challenges the rigid "my way or the highway" mentality, advocating instead for a more flexible approach that values and empowers team members to utilize their own ideas and methods. The chapter highlights the experience of a leader who shifted from directing people towards solutions they deemed "better" to empowering others to find their own way. This change stemmed from the realization that people's motivation and commitment often flourish significantly when they are given the autonomy to pursue solutions using their unique perspectives and approaches, even if they differ from the leader's preferred method.

This empowerment fosters greater ownership and motivation within the team. Servant-Minded Leadership recognizes that the leader does not need to possess the single "best" solution for every challenge. Instead, the focus shifts to facilitating inclusive, team-driven solutions. Valuing diverse approaches and collaborating with team members, even when their methods seem different or potentially less efficient at first glance, builds trust and leverages the collective intelligence of the group. This mindset allows leaders to move beyond rigid control, embracing collaboration and acknowledging the value in different ways of achieving a goal.

**Key Takeaways:**

1. **Genuine empowerment fosters greater ownership and motivation.**

2. **Leaders don't always need the "best" solution—they need inclusive, team-driven solutions.**

3. **Servant-minded leadership values diversity and collaboration over rigid control.**

# Summary of Chapter 16

*Proper Nouns* ~ (Page 81)

Servant-Minded Leaders recognize that their team members are not just generic resources or "nouns" but unique individuals, referred to metaphorically as "proper nouns." This perspective challenges the common feeling among employees of being treated as mere numbers, a dehumanizing experience for many workers. Instead, Servant-Minded Leadership emphasizes the importance of genuinely knowing people, moving beyond simple facts about them to understanding who they are as individuals. This involves cultivating authentic care that, while remaining professional and appropriate, fosters personal connection.

Putting this principle into practice means actively engaging with team members by asking good questions, listening with a true intent to understand, and remembering important details about their lives, such as family events, personal challenges, or significant milestones. This genuine interest goes beyond performative "active listening"; it stems from a sincere desire to show that each person is valued and worthy of dignity. Demonstrating care through thoughtful engagement, like following up on a past conversation point or acknowledging a personal event, builds trust and reinforces that leaders see and appreciate their team members for who they are, not just for their function.

**Key Takeaways:**

1. **Servant-Minded Leaders see team members as unique individuals, not just functions.**

2. **Genuine connection requires moving beyond facts about people to truly knowing them.**

3. **Practical steps include: asking, listening, and remembering personal details.**

# *Summary of Chapter 17*

*Servant-Minded Leaders Have Mentors* ~ (Page 91)

Servant-Minded Leaders understand the critical role of mentorship in their development. Unlike coaches, who may offer more structured guidance, mentors are individuals who have already walked the path the leader aspires to travel, providing insights based on lived experience rather than theory alone. A mentor offers an invaluable third-party perspective, helping leaders stay true to the principles of Servant-Minded Leadership when navigating complex situations and providing discernment in processing thoughts. They serve as a sounding board, aiding in the processing of ideas and offering crucial insights needed for leading others effectively.

Finding the right mentor is a deliberate process guided by key questions: identifying those one genuinely respects, determining who among them has achieved the goals one aims for, and assessing willingness to invest time in the leader's success. Respect is paramount in this search, and finding someone ahead on the desired path ensures relevant guidance. While asking for mentorship can be daunting, the effort yields immeasurable rewards, including external perspective, help refining leadership skills, and valuable wisdom gained from experience. Mentorship provides a deeper level of support compared to coaching, essential for the ongoing growth and effectiveness of a Servant-Minded Leader.

**Key Takeaways:**

1. **Mentors provide outside perspective grounded in wisdom and experience.**

2. **A good mentor has already achieved the goals you are working toward.**

3. **Effective mentorship involves trust, respect, and a shared commitment to growth.**

# Summary of Chapter 18

*Servant-Minded Leaders Get Started ~ (Page 97)*

Many aspiring leaders feel they are not yet "ready" to take on leadership roles. However, the journey of becoming a Servant-Minded Leader begins not with perfect preparedness, but with the decision to simply get started now. Leadership development requires persistence, not perfection, and embracing the ongoing learning process. A fundamental step in this journey is cultivating a genuine love for people, ensuring that team members feel valued, appreciated, and recognize their contributions matter. This authentic care should be palpable in daily interactions, demonstrating that their well-being is a priority.

Moving beyond intentions requires concrete action. Servant-Minded Leaders set simple, actionable goals to guide their progress. A recommended method for setting effective goals is the TNT approach: Time-Oriented goals have deadlines, Narrowed goals are specific and targeted, and Temperate goals are challenging yet realistic. Setting goals using this method provides clarity, allows for tracking progress, and empowers leaders to achieve tangible results. By committing to start, nurturing a love for others, and setting actionable goals, leaders embark on the transformative path of Servant-Minded Leadership.

**Key Takeaways:**

1. **Leadership begins with daily, intentional choices rooted in love and service.**

2. **Genuine love for people fosters respect and drives meaningful impact.**

3. **Achievable, time-bound goals are essential to translating principles into practice.**

# *Summary of Chapter 19*

*Doing What it Takes as a Servant-Minded Leader* ~ (Page 101)

Deciding to act is just the beginning. True leadership requires more than intentions—it demands action, accountability, and visible commitment. Decisions without follow-through change nothing. The gap between aspiring leaders and effective leaders is bridged by execution, persistence, and willingness to embrace the work.

**Steps to Action:**

Commit through a meaningful ritual:

- Physically engage in a symbolic act, such as drawing a line in the sand and stepping over it to signify your commitment to Servant-Minded Leadership.
- Use affirmations to solidify your intention and reflect on the journey ahead.

Make your commitment public:

- Share your decision with your team, mentor, or trusted associates to solidify your accountability. Verbalizing your goals amplifies their power and momentum.

Establish accountability:

- Select accountability partners who care about your growth, speak truthfully, and maintain confidentiality. Their feedback will help sustain your commitment.

Initiate immediate changes:

- Don't wait for the perfect moment or formal approval to make personal adjustments. Start today by implementing small but impactful changes aligned with your goals.

Taking these steps transforms desire into action, ensuring that leadership becomes a reality, not just an aspiration.

# Summary of Chapter 20

*I Love You* ~ (Page 111)

A fundamental, though sometimes debated, principle of Servant-Minded Leadership is the concept of genuinely loving one's team. True leadership moves beyond theoretical discussion to actively living out principles. Love in leadership is guided by two key principles: first, doing unto your team as they would like you to do unto them, and second, doing unto your team what is best for them. This rephrasing of the traditional Golden Rule emphasizes the need for leaders to understand and cater to the specific needs and preferences of their individual team members, rather than simply treating everyone as the leader themselves would wish to be treated.

The principle of doing what is best for the team acknowledges that sometimes the most caring actions involve challenges, growth, or difficult feedback, which may not be what employees initially desire. Real love in leadership prioritizes long-term well-being and development over immediate comfort or satisfaction. Leaders must sometimes guide their teams through difficult changes or increased expectations because it is ultimately in the team's best interest, even if it causes temporary discomfort. This requires leaders to move beyond generic kindness to personalized care and a commitment to fostering genuine growth.

## Key Takeaways:

1. **Authentic love for the team is a core principle of Servant-Minded Leadership.**

2. **Balancing team desires with their best interests demonstrates true servant-minded love.**

3. **Leadership is an act of service that prioritizes the team's growth over personal convenience.**

# Summary of Chapter 21

*I'm Here for You! ~* (Page 117)

Just as individuals make time for the relationships and activities they value most, Servant-Minded Leaders demonstrate their commitment to their team by making themselves available. Time is presented as the "currency of love," highlighting that claiming a lack of time for team members contradicts the principle of genuinely caring for them. Moving beyond the outdated model of aloof and inaccessible leadership, Servant-Minded Leaders ensure their presence and accessibility are felt by their team, proving through action that their team is a priority.

Three practical steps can help leaders prove their availability. First, scheduling dedicated "open-door" time signals a predictable window for team members to connect. Second, creating an inviting and open physical or virtual space, coupled with giving undivided attention, encourages people to approach. Third, celebrating and positively reinforcing those who utilize the leader's availability validates their initiative and encourages others to follow suit. While being consistently available may not always be easy due to competing demands, it is a necessary demonstration of authentic care and a cornerstone of Servant-Minded Leadership, showing the team, they are valued.

**Key Takeaways:**

1. **Servant-Minded Leaders prioritize their team's needs by making time for them.**

2. **Time is seen as the "currency of love" in leadership.**

3. **Practical steps like scheduling open-door time, creating inviting spaces, and celebrating engagement demonstrate availability.**

# Summary of Chapter 22

*Are You Even Listening?* ~ (Page 123)

A fundamental yet often overlooked practice in effective leadership, and the third practical step for a Servant-Minded Leader, is to genuinely listen. This goes far beyond merely allowing words to be heard; it means listening with the explicit intent to understand what is being communicated and being open to the possibility of learning something new. Unlike passively waiting for one's turn to speak or preparing a response, Servant-Minded Leaders actively engage with the speaker's message, seeking to fully grasp their perspective.

The degree to which a leader listens reflects how much they value the person speaking and their input. Just as individuals pay close attention when navigating an unfamiliar place or ordering in a new restaurant because they believe the guide or waitstaff possesses valuable information, effective leaders listen intently because they believe their team members have something important to share. This intentional, understanding-focused listening is a clear mark of a Servant-Minded Leader, stemming directly from a foundation of love and respect for the people they lead and a recognition that they do not know everything.

**Key Takeaways:**

1. **Listening is more than hearing—it's about understanding and valuing the speaker.**

2. **Assuming we already know leads to disengagement; curiosity fosters connection.**

3. **Servant-Minded Leaders listen with humility and a genuine desire to learn.**

# Summary of Chapter 23

*Si, Ja, Oui, Sim, Evet, Tak, Da, 是的, はい, Yes* ~ (Page 127)

A core principle of Servant-Minded Leadership involves a shift from a mindset of control and being constantly "right" to one of collaboration and openness: "finding the yes." This approach recognizes that leadership success is not contingent on having all the answers or ensuring tasks are done exactly one's own way. Instead, effectiveness increases when leaders accept that their method is not the only or necessarily the best one. Implementing "finding the yes" requires understanding the people being led – their motivations, needs, and aspirations – building on the principle of seeing them as "proper nouns."

By adopting a perspective of seeking possibilities rather than problems, leaders can encourage ownership and collaboration. Three primary strategies facilitate this: simply saying yes and ensuring follow-through when an idea aligns with objectives; adapting ideas to make them feasible, addressing the underlying need behind a request; and empowering a team member to take the lead on their suggestion, fostering growth and shared responsibility. This practice, rooted in love, time, and listening, allows leaders to cultivate an environment where innovation and contribution are genuinely embraced, moving beyond the "my way or the highway" approach.

## Key Takeaways:

1. **Saying "yes" validates and empowers team members, fostering creativity and morale.**

2. **Effective leaders balance wisdom with openness, avoiding assumptions about what won't work.**

3. **Finding the yes involves collaboration, alternative solutions, and empowering individuals to implement their ideas.**

# Summary of Chapter 24

*OK, So What's Next? ~ (Page 135)*

Completing the journey of understanding Servant-Minded Leadership principles is merely a step; the real work lies in applying them consistently, recognizing that growth is a continuous process. A significant challenge is "ascent without activation," where individuals agree with concepts but fail to implement them. Therefore, the crucial next step after reading is ensuring that the principles learned are being effectively applied in real-world leadership. Obtaining objective insight into one's application is vital before seeking new knowledge, highlighting the importance of humility in leadership development.

This objective insight is best gained through feedback, which is presented as an essential tool for refinement and growth. Obtaining honest feedback can be difficult due to inherent power dynamics, but creating a safe environment for it is paramount. A three-step process is recommended: initially making feedback anonymous to ensure safety, celebrating participation to encourage contribution, and taking immediate, visible action based on the feedback to build trust and demonstrate genuine listening. This foundation can lead to more comprehensive feedback models, like the 360°, furthering a leader's transformation from inspiration to impactful action through continuous application and learning.

**Key Takeaways:**

1. **Feedback is vital for sustained leadership growth and fostering trust within teams.**

2. **The 360° feedback model ensures balanced perspectives from all organizational levels.**

3. **Growth is actualized when feedback leads to visible, meaningful action.**

# The Conclusion

Well, you did it! You've read the entire book. I know it isn't that long, but it still isn't easy to read. I know that there is a lot contained in these few pages.

This is, of course, NOT the end of the journey! Growth does not stop because we finish a book! There is still a great deal for both you and me to learn and engage as we seek to be true Servant-Minded Leaders.

But our journey through this book is over, and it is time for us both to start new projects! If you would like additional resources that are of the Servant-Minded Leadership mindset, I would invite you to find us online, using the QR code below or via our website: www.servantmindedleadership.com. There, you will find resources such as blogs, assessments, videos, etc., that are all free and designed to empower you in your leadership journey.

And, of course, if ever we can directly support you or your team via events, coaching, or certifications, please do not hesitate to reach out to us. Mention that you reached out after reading this book for a special offer on any services!

For now, I wish you all the best as you seek to make a dynamic impact by effectively engaging with your team and changing the world one person at a time!

# Acknowledgments

If we doubled this book, there would not be enough pages to acknowledge all of the people who deserve it. Even as I write this, I fear that I will fail to remember someone who has had a profound impact on my life. Thanks to God for the gift of grace I experience every day, but so often fail to represent well.

Thank you to my wife for her unwavering love and support as I seek to do my little bit of good in the world.

And to my best friend and brother, Josh, who has been a bulwark of support and help to me for as long as I can recall, I don't have enough words...

I am also deeply grateful for my parents who gave me a solid foundation (that I found every way to jump off of), the mentors I've been privileged to learn from (when I actually stop talking), the friends who choose to continue with me (despite my terrible jokes), and the many, many, many people with whom I have been so honored to share in part of this journey we call life. I learn from each of you, I hold you in the highest regard, and I love you!

I firmly believe that I am a turtle on a fence-post (If you ever see one, I guarantee they did not get there by themselves). I stand on the shoulders of giants, and am humbled to have the opportunity to lift up others.

To each person I've been fortunate enough to cross paths with—especially those listed above—I appreciate you, and this book is because of you!

# About the Author

Jon Antonucci is a leadership expert, keynote speaker, and founder of SML Consultive, a firm committed to empowering frontline and mid-level leaders through servant-minded, love-based leadership. With over two decades of experience, Jon has led diverse teams across corporate, nonprofit, and international arenas—holding roles from Training Manager to Director of Revenue—while consistently driving performance, engagement, and cultural transformation.

As a sought-after consultant and speaker, Jon has worked with organizations to recession-proof their operations by investing in overlooked but critical leadership tiers. His strategies have helped companies reduce turnover, improve morale, and unlock the untapped potential of middle management. In 2023, he launched SML Consultive to scale this mission, offering hands-on coaching, workshops, and keynotes that challenge conventional leadership models and prioritize service, presence, and authenticity.

Jon holds a Master's Degree in Theology and brings a rare blend of real-world leadership, academic depth, and transformational insight. He has been featured in leadership podcasts, business forums, and national media for his unique approach to culture-building and values-driven influence.

He currently lives in South Carolina with his wife and continues to mentor rising leaders while championing organizational change that begins with the heart.

www.ingramcontent.com/pod-product-compliance
Lightning Source LLC
Chambersburg PA
CBHW060543210326
41519CB00014B/3331